C000257338

MICKEY MOUSE MUSEUM

THE STORY OF AN ICON

First published in the UK in 2018
by Studio Press Books,
an imprint of Kings Road Publishing,
part of Bonnier Books UK,
The Plaza, 535 King's Road,
London, SW10 0SZ

www.studiopressbooks.co.uk
www.bonnierbooks.co.uk

Printed in Italy

3 5 7 9 10 8 6 4 2

ISBN 978-1-78741-359-7

Written by Nicole Corse
Edited by Emma Drage
Designed by Rob Ward

Welcome to the

MICKEY MOUSE MUSEUM

PREFACE

After 90 years, Mickey Mouse is as popular and as relevant as ever, his familiar form instantly recognisable around the world. Yet, despite his astounding success, he still possesses that humble personality that endears him to all of us.

At first, Mickey Mouse was simply an animated character who, through his playful actions on screen, resonated with movie audiences. He was an 'everyman' with whom they could identify; through Mickey Mouse, they could see themselves on screen, trying to make their way through life as best they can. Audiences could see in him an optimistic reflection of their own values.

Over the years, Mickey's look and style may have changed, but his simplicity and his sincerity have stayed the same. Throughout many artistic interpretations, from the simple 'rubber hose' style animation imparted by Ub Iwerks to the rounder, more weighty and appealing form instilled by the hand of Freddie Moore, to even his more contemporary designs, Mickey Mouse remains, unmistakably, Mickey Mouse. In this volume, *Mickey Mouse Museum*, you will enjoy an amazing collection of art and memories of this most celebrated figure.

Mickey maintains an irrepressible connection with every generation. "When people laugh at Mickey Mouse," Walt once said, "it is because he is so human". In the spotlight of his anniversary celebrations, Mickey himself would be quite modest and likely warble a gentle, "Aw shucks!" Ever since Mickey Mouse first sparkled upon that silver screen with his debut in *Steamboat Willie,* he has not only entertained us and made us laugh, he has also made us look at ourselves and at the world around us. In doing so, he has made us realise there is a little bit of Mickey Mouse in all of us.

Fox Carney
Manager of research at the Disney Animation Research Library (ARL)

SECTION 1

ENTRANCE

Walt Disney
Timeline
Mickey Mouse

WALT DISNEY

Walter Elias Disney was born on 5 December, 1901 in Chicago, Illinois. Disney spent the majority of his early childhood in the small town of Marceline, Missouri until his parents, Elias and Flora, relocated to Kansas City, Missouri in 1911. Walt was the youngest of four boys, followed by a younger sister named Ruth.

In October 1919, Walt got a job at Pesmen-Rubin Commercial Art Studio as an apprentice commercial artist[1]. Although the position only lasted a few months, it was an important moment in his career as this was where he met Ub Iwerks, who would eventually help him to bring Mickey Mouse to the silver screen. In late January 1920, Walt was hired at the Kansas City Slide Company, where he discovered animation. From there he opened his first company, Laugh-O-gram Films, Inc., which was ultimately unsuccessful. However, before it went out of business, Walt was able to make a pilot film, titled *Alice's Wonderland*, which was an early example of animation and live action combined.

With the recent failure of his business, Walt needed a change of scenery. In July of 1923, he boarded a train to Los Angeles, California, where his older brother Roy was living at the time. Soon, Roy and Walt formed the Disney Brothers Cartoon Studio. Walt's *Alice's Wonderland* sample reel caught the interest of a New York distributor named Margaret Winkler. She commissioned the *Alice Comedies* series, and the Disney brothers were in business.

With new projects being started up, Ub Iwerks joined Walt out West. On 13 July, 1925, Walt married Lillian Bounds, one of the inkers working at the studio. In early 1926, the Disney brothers moved their studio to a new facility and renamed it the Walt Disney Studio. It was the beginning of an incredible journey that would impact the world for generations to come.

KEY TO PLATE

1: Illustration of Walt Disney with some characters

1962

This image appeared on a fan card that would be mailed in response to fan mail received at the studio.

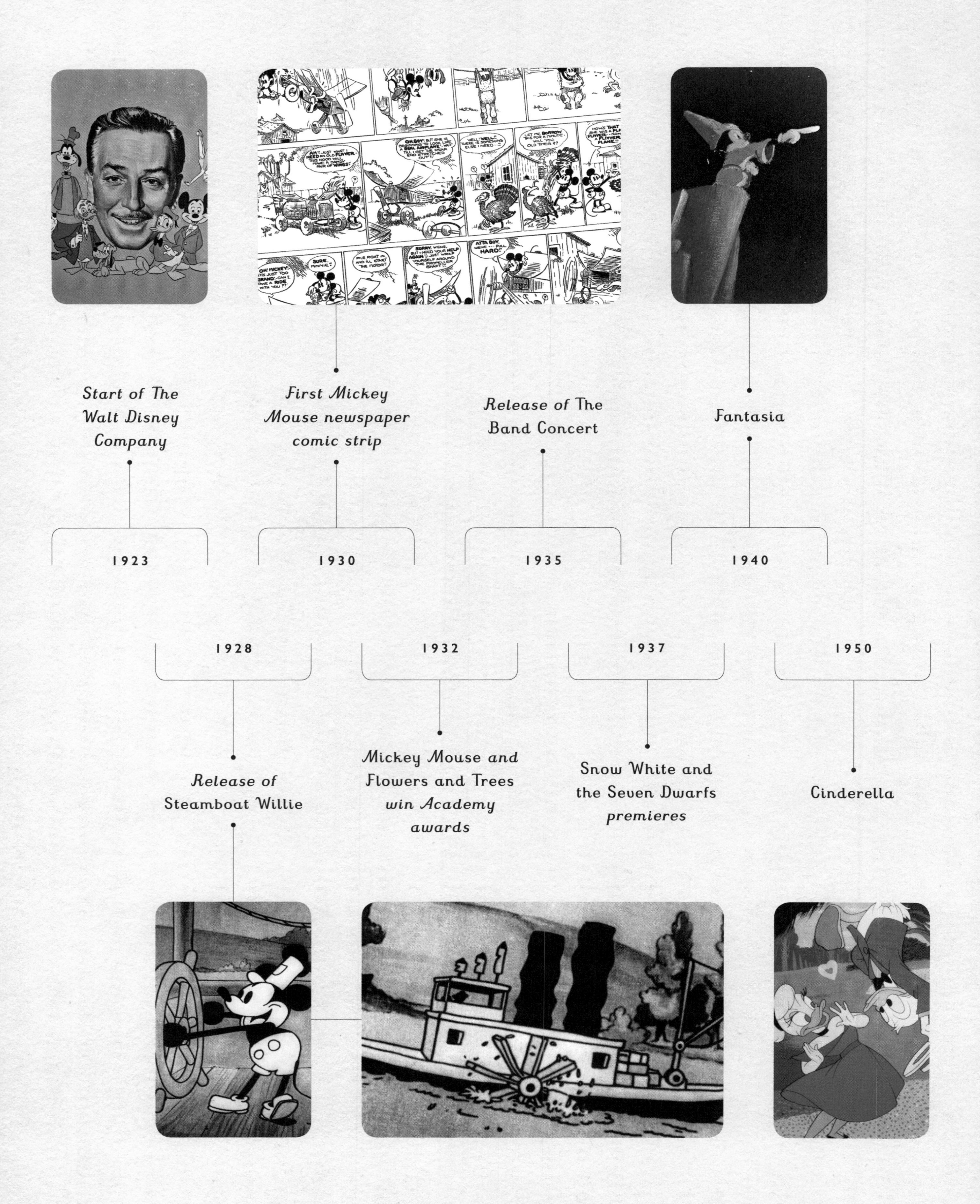

1923
Start of The Walt Disney Company
1928
Release of Steamboat Willie
1930
First Mickey Mouse newspaper comic strip
1932
Mickey Mouse and Flowers and Trees win Academy awards
1935
Release of The Band Concert
1937
Snow White and the Seven Dwarfs premieres
1940
Fantasia
1950
Cinderella

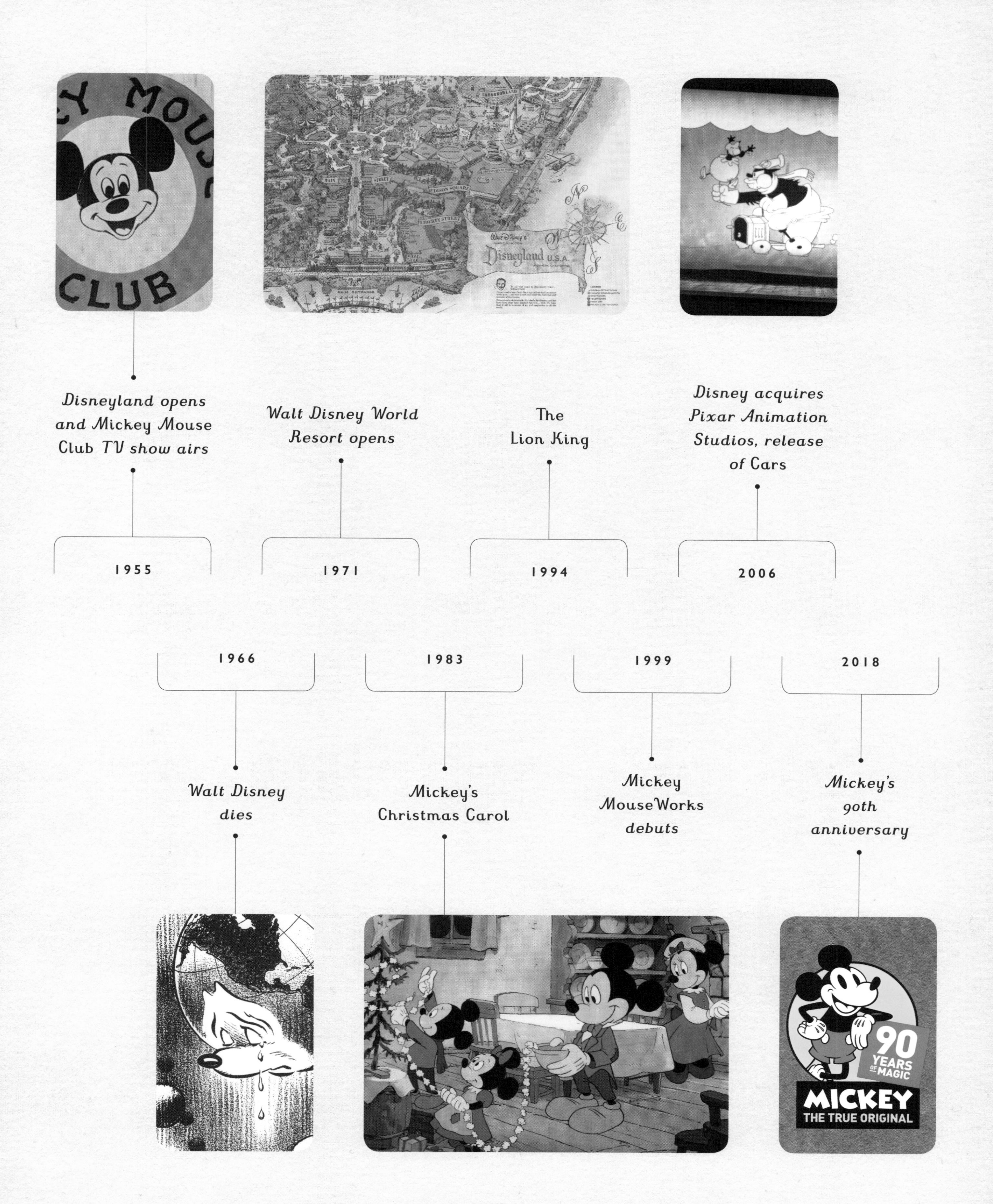

CLUB
Disneyland U.S.A.
1955
Disneyland opens and Mickey Mouse Club TV show airs
1966
Walt Disney dies
1971
Walt Disney World Resort opens
1983
Mickey's Christmas Carol
1994
The Lion King
1999
Mickey MouseWorks debuts
2006
Disney acquires Pixar Animation Studios, release of Cars
2018
Mickey's 90th anniversary
90 YEARS OF MAGIC
MICKEY
THE TRUE ORIGINAL

MICKEY MOUSE

Mickey Mouse is a name recognised by almost every person in the world. American novelist John Updike, in a piece titled "The Mystery of Mickey Mouse" described Mickey as "the most persistent and pervasive figment of American popular culture in this century."[2]

Since his public debut in the animated short *Steamboat Willie* in 1928, Mickey Mouse has appeared in books, comics, magazines, movies, video games, television shows, feature films and on the radio. His image dominates the consumer goods landscape through clothes, toys and food products. Throughout the decades, Mickey has adapted to advancements in animation and entertainment. He has accomplished all of this while also appearing at Disney Parks since Disneyland first opened in 1955.

Mickey's career began in 1928, after Walt lost a character named Oswald the Lucky Rabbit. Walt went to New York to renegotiate his Oswald contract only to discover that Universal, his distributor, not Walt, owned the rights to the character. Although it was a crushing disappointment, Walt got straight to work in thinking of a replacement character on the train ride back to California.

Even though Mickey may be small, he's an adventurer who inspires everyone's inner child to experience the world around them with delight. An icon that has touched the hearts of several generations, for 90 years, Mickey has been an endearing symbol of optimism, happiness and magic.

KEY TO PLATE

***1:* Mickey Mouse**
circa March 1928
One of the earliest known images of Mickey Mouse. This sketch is attributed to Ub Iwerks.

***2:* Minnie Mouse**
To the right of Mickey is one of the earliest sketches of Minnie Mouse.

***3:* Plane Crazy**
This turkey tail seen on the far right appeared in *Plane Crazy,* Mickey's first film to be animated.

***4:* Plane Crazy**
A similar horseshoe to this one is given to Mickey by Minnie in *Plane Crazy.*

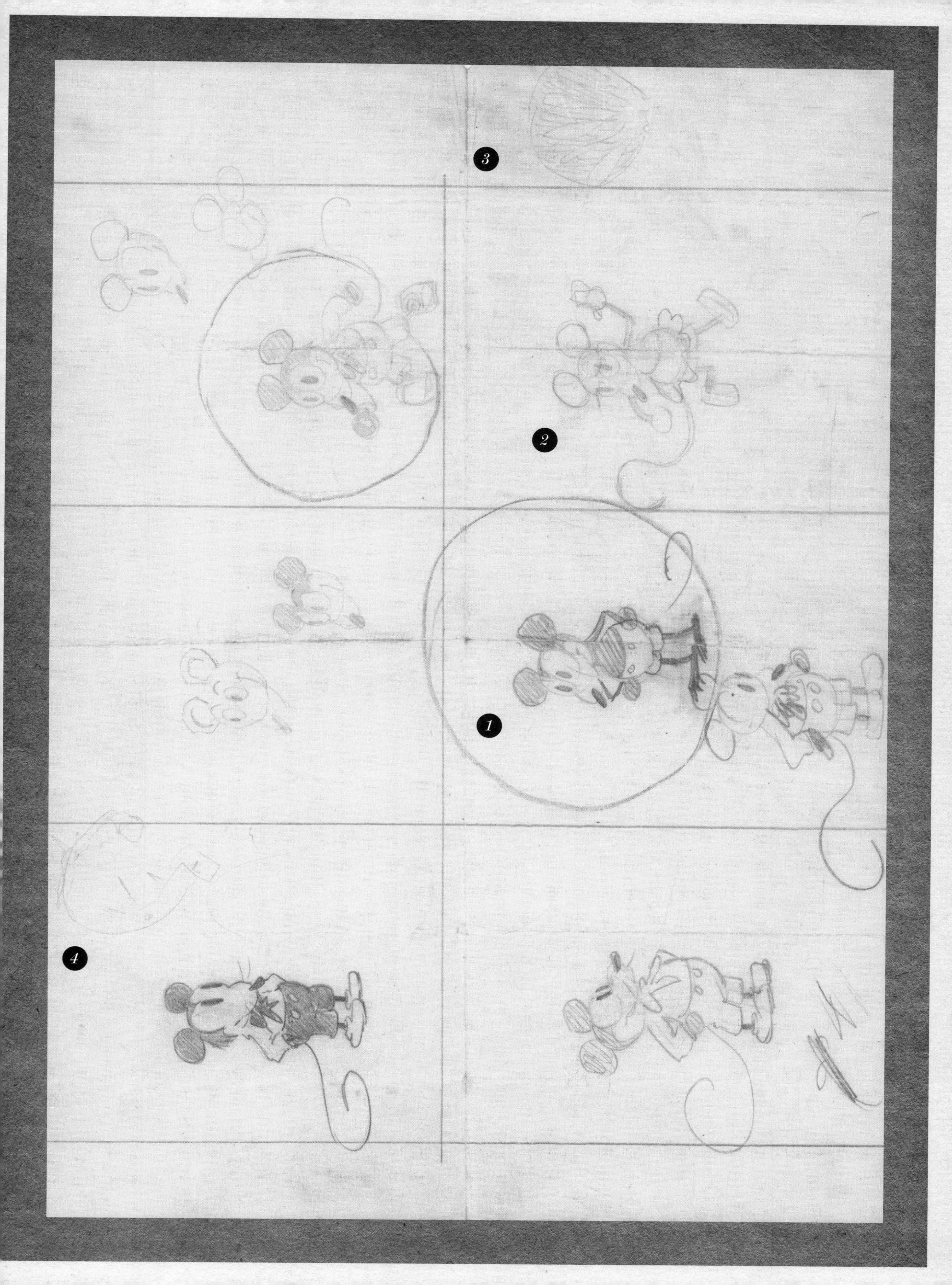

SECTION 2

IT WAS ALL STARTED BY A MOUSE

Oswald the Lucky Rabbit
Rebuilding
From Mortimer to Mickey
A Star was Born
In My Image

OSWALD THE LUCKY RABBIT

Before there was Mickey, there was Oswald the Lucky Rabbit, a character that would eventually prove to be rather unlucky for Walt Disney. During the mid-1920s, Felix the Cat was enjoying a lot of success and audience interest in the *Alice Comedies* was declining. With the success of the *Alice Comedies,* Charles Mintz, who had married Margaret Winkler and taken over operations of her film distribution business, had entered into an agreement with Universal and hired Walt to develop an animated character to compete with Felix the Cat. That character would become Oswald the Lucky Rabbit.

Walt, wanting to impress Universal, completed the first Oswald short, *Poor Papa*, in about two weeks. Unfortunately, Universal and Charles Mintz disliked it and Walt was sent back to the drawing board (the short would end up getting released much later, in June 1928).[3] *Trolley Troubles* was the first of Walt's Oswald shorts to see theatrical release, in early September 1927. To much fanfare, it was a hit and Walt went on to animate many more Oswald shorts. To keep up with this demand, Walt had increased the size of his staff by the end of 1927.

In the Spring of 1928, Walt took a cross-country train trip with his wife, Lillian, to renegotiate his contract with Charles Mintz. Walt wanted to be able to invest in new technologies and grow the potential of Oswald. When Walt began the discussion he was shocked to find that not only did Mintz offer him a salary decrease, but also that if Walt did not agree to the terms, he would lose Oswald since Universal retained the rights to the character. In addition, Mintz had signed agreements with almost all of Walt's staff with a few exceptions, Ub Iwerks among them. Walt decided to end his dealings with Mintz and return to California.

KEY TO PLATE

1, 2, 3: ***Frames from* The Mechanical Cow, *the fourth Oswald cartoon***
Released 1927
In this short, Oswald tries to wake up a mechanical cow. He pushes the cow down a slide and it lands on roller skates. Oswald sells milk until they encounter a female rabbit, who is thrown into a car by a brute.

4, 5: ***Frames from* The Ol' Swimmin' 'ole**
Released 6 February, 1928

REBUILDING

With the loss of Oswald, Walt had to find a new character to focus his talents on, and quickly. When Walt returned to Hollywood, with the help of Ub, and several other trusted staff members, they got to work on their next character, Mickey Mouse. Immediately, production began on the first Mickey short, *Plane Crazy,* although it would not be released until 1929 after *Steamboat Willie* and *The Gallopin' Gaucho* premiered. *Plane Crazy* featured a shoeless Mickey and his leading partner, Minnie, who embark on an adventurous plane ride. *Plane Crazy* was shown to test audiences in late Spring of 1928,[4] at the same time as Disney applied to register Mickey Mouse as a trademark with the US Patent Office.

Plane Crazy opens with several animals hard at work. Soon, Mickey hops aboard a crude plane his animal friends have built, the plane is wound up and off he goes! The ride is less than smooth and ends in a crash. Mickey feels defeated, but he uses a nearby car, attaches a propeller and with a few adjustments only Mickey could perform, he has a new aeroplane. Minnie comes along and Mickey invites her aboard as his passenger. The plane takes off, but then they hit a bump and Mickey is expelled from his seat. Minnie is now seated in the back of the plane, which takes off on a journey of its own. Mickey chases after the runaway plane and eventually catches up to it. Minnie jumps out of the plane, using her clothing as a parachute. Mickey lands with a crash but is ultimately unscathed.

After animation was finalised on *Plane Crazy,* Ub immediately began working on a second short, *The Gallopin' Gaucho* which also wasn't released until after *Steamboat Willie*. In this short, Mickey takes a ride on an ostrich, where he meets Minnie and dances with her. Then, Peg Leg Pete takes her and runs off with her. A chase ensues, ending at a building where Minnie cries from a top-storey window. Mickey uses his tail as a lasso and makes his way up to Minnie. He encounters Peg Leg Pete and defeats him, saving the day. This was the first time Peg Leg Pete was used as a villain for Mickey.

With the release of *The Jazz Singer* in October 1927, Walt saw a new frontier for animation and needed to leave these two Mickey shorts on the drawing table for the time being. Walt set his sights on sound and never looked back.

KEY TO PLATE

***1:* Promotional poster art for Plane Crazy**
Circa 1929
Promotional poster art for *Plane Crazy* attributed to Ub Iwerks, 1929. After the warm reception for *Steamboat Willie,* sound would be added to the first two Mickey cartoons. This promotional poster was for the version with sound, as emphasised under Mickey's name.

***2:* Illustration from Plane Crazy**
Released 1929
Mickey is studying a book titled *How to Fly,* featuring images of Charles Lindbergh, who achieved the first solo plane flight over the Atlantic Ocean on 21 May, 1927. Mickey's left leg is behind the book he is peering at. This image is from the first scene in which Mickey's face is visible.

***3:* Illustration from Plane Crazy**
Released 1929
This image is from the first scene in which Minnie makes an appearance. Mickey invites her aboard his plane. Shortly after take-off, Mickey is ejected from the plane and Minnie takes off on a wild ride.

A WALT DISNEY COMIC
by UB IWERKS
RECORDED BY Powers CINEPHONE SYSTEM

1

2

3

FROM MORTIMER TO MICKEY

As with most legendary figures, there are multiple versions of the story of Mickey's true beginnings. Some speculate that the idea for Mickey was born from Walt's interactions with friendly mice at early workplaces in Kansas City. Or perhaps it was the noises made by the train during Walt and Lillian's return journey to the West Coast after losing Oswald. One thing is certain, Mickey was born out of a necessity to fill the hole Oswald left behind.

In an interview with *Windsor Magazine* in October 1931 titled "Mickey Mouse: How He Was Born", Walt said, "Why did I choose a mouse for my principal character? Principally because I needed a small animal. I couldn't use a rabbit, because there already was a rabbit on the screen. So I decided upon a mouse, as I have always thought they were very interesting little creatures [...] While returning from a visit to New York, I plotted out the first story, which was later to be released to the public as *Plane Crazy*."[6]

When Walt and Lillian arrived in California after that train ride from the East Coast on Sunday, 18 March, 1928, they rallied the troops, and got to work. Originally, Mortimer Mouse was the chosen name for the new character, but Lillian Disney disapproved of the moniker. She told *McCall's Magazine* in an interview in February 1953 that she exclaimed, "Mortimer is a horrible name for a mouse!"[7] It was soon decided that the mouse's name would be Mickey. But the name Mortimer did not slip into obscurity. Mortimer was reimagined as Minnie's wealthy uncle in the *Mickey Mouse* comic strip in September 1930 and was reinvented again as a rat-like villain in several animated appearances.

KEY TO PLATE

***1:* Illustration from the interior of Mickey Mouse Book**
Published October 1930
This illustration accompanied a story about how Mickey met Walt.[5]

***2:* Birthday card for Elias Disney, born 6 February, 1859**
circa February 1926
The inscription reads: "Wishing you a happy birthday – Dad – your Hollywood kids –" The calendar is titled "The Month of Important Birthdays" and lists Abraham Lincoln and George Washington's birthdays. This card features three mice, one of whom wears gloves, perhaps an early inspiration for Mickey.

1

FEBRUARY
ELIAS DISNEY -1859-
ABE LINCOLN -1809-
GEO. WASHINGTON -1732-
THE MONTH OF IM TANT
BIRTHDAYS
Wishing you a happy birthday — Dad
— your Hollywood Kids —

2

A STAR WAS BORN

With the release of *The Jazz Singer* in October 1927, Disney was inspired to apply the same synchronisation of sound used in that film to his animated shorts. It was considered a risk, since at the time audiences were not accustomed to animated characters having a voice. Even theatre owners were unsure if 'talkies' would have a lasting presence in common culture.[8]

Having completed the first two silent Mickey shorts *Plane Crazy* and *The Gallopin' Gaucho*, Disney forged ahead on a third Mickey short, although it would be the first one released, *Steamboat Willie*, this time with the intention of sound synchronisation from the beginning.

Mickey Mouse made his debut on 18 November, 1928 with the premiere of *Steamboat Willie* at the Colony Theatre in New York City. After seeing the short and realising its potential, Harry Reichenbach, who managed the Colony Theatre at that time, offered to screen *Steamboat Willie* for two weeks before a feature named *Gang War*.

The day after the premiere, Mordaunt Hall, one of the earliest movie critics for *The New York Times*, gave Mickey his first review in print, calling *Steamboat Willie* "an ingenious piece of work with a good deal of fun". That review would be the first of many throughout Mickey's illustrious career.

KEY TO PLATE

1: **Steamboat Willie**
1928
In this scene drawn by Ub Iwerks that has now become iconic in cinematic history, audiences are introduced to Mickey Mouse. The first sound Mickey emits is a whistle to the tune of "Steamboat Bill", the theme song from Buster Keaton's *Steamboat Bill, Jr.*, which *Steamboat Willie* borrowed inspiration from.

2: ***The opening image of* Steamboat Willie**
The silhouette of Mickey appears underneath the three whistles. As the steamboat chugs along, the sounds take on a musical quality. In his debut role, Mickey plays a deckhand, who acts for a moment as if he were captain of the ship, whistling and tapping his foot.

3: ***Title card for* Steamboat Willie**
Through the end of the decade, Mickey and Minnie appear in their original title card design. At the start of the 1930s, Mickey and Minnie's eyes shift towards the audience. The stripes on Mickey's shorts disappear, as does his hat. Both Walt and Ub's names appear here with the larger font size used for Ub's name, suggesting his important contribution to the creation of Mickey Mouse.

1

2

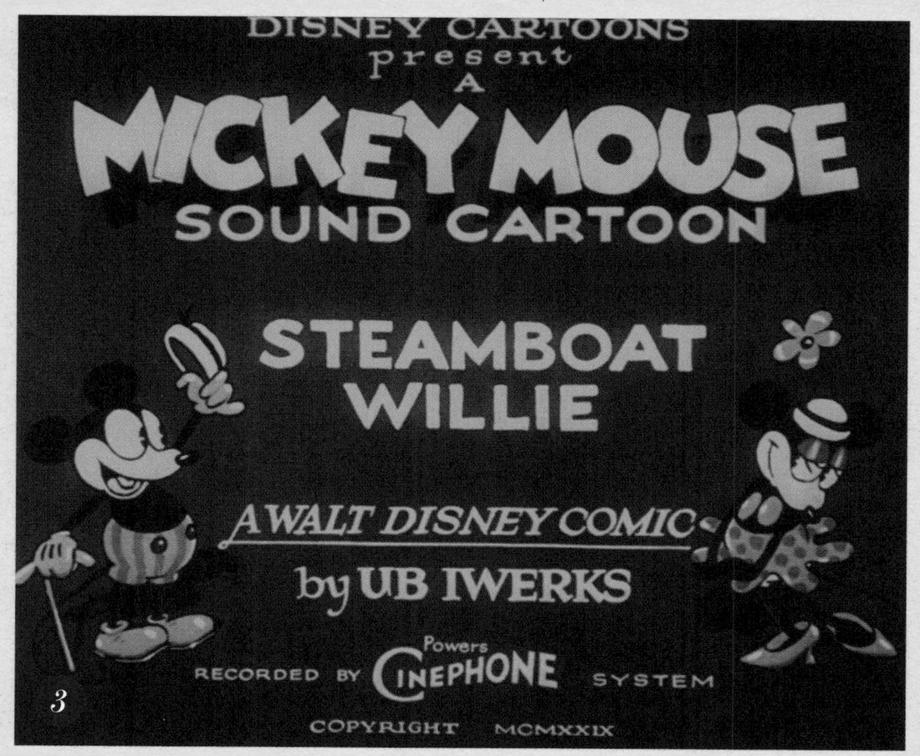
DISNEY CARTOONS
present
A
MICKEY MOUSE
SOUND CARTOON
STEAMBOAT
WILLIE
A WALT DISNEY COMIC
by UB IWERKS
RECORDED BY Powers CINEPHONE SYSTEM
COPYRIGHT MCMXXIX
3

IN MY IMAGE

From the beginning, Walt and Mickey were intertwined. Born from Walt's mind, Mickey became an extension of his creator, with Walt predominately lending his own voice to the character from his inception until the late 1940s. Mickey was the type of character who could get out of any situation. Walt was the keeper of Mickey's consciousness. In several interviews, animators recall Walt responding to story points by saying, "Mickey wouldn't do that."

Walt's love of Charlie Chaplin and other actors popular during the time period infused Mickey's character with humorous traits and eternal optimism throughout his first appearances. Disney said in a 1931 interview with *The American Magazine,* "I think we were rather indebted to Charlie Chaplin for the idea. We wanted something appealing, and we thought of a tiny bit of a mouse that would have something of the wistfulness of Chaplin... a little fellow trying to do the best he could."[9]

As Walt focused more on his home life, so too did Mickey. In early 1927, the Disneys brought home a chow chow named Sunnee to join their family.[10] Four years later, Mickey got his very own canine companion, Pluto. In 1933, Walt and Lillian's first daughter, Diane, was born, which likely helped to inspire more domestic tales for Mickey.

In 1936, the Disneys welcomed a second daughter, Sharon, into their home. Walt's success was inextricably linked to Mickey's success and both of their stories would be forever intertwined.

KEY TO PLATE

1: Walt's self-portrait by Charles Boyer for the cover of Backstage Magazine
Summer 1978
This issue also covered Mickey's 50th anniversary. A statement included on the inside front cover reads: "When Mickey made his screen debut in 1928, magazines such as the *Saturday Evening Post* and *Collier's* were debuting original works by the great Norman Rockwell. Our Backstage cover, brushed by the expert hand of our Creative Service's Department's Charles Boyer, is based on one of Rockwell's humorous-looks-at-life-on-canvas, in this case the artist attempting a self-portrait." Norman Rockwell's *Triple Self-Portrait* originally appeared on the 13 February, 1960 cover of the *Saturday Evening Post.* The artist, Charles Boyer, made a few adjustments, replacing Norman Rockwell with Walt and Mickey. A few, additional subtle changes made by the artist includes adding Mickey to the glass near the mirror on the left-hand side of the image. He added a realistic mouse to the floor and replaced the topmost part of the easel with Mickey Mouse ears.

BACKSTAGE

Founded A°. D. 1955 by W. E. Disney

Illustrated Semi-Annually

Summer 1978

SECTION 3

THE FRIENDS

MINNIE MOUSE

Ever since there was Mickey, there was Minnie. Minnie Mouse made her silver screen debut alongside Mickey in *Steamboat Willie* in 1928. She also played the leading lady in both *Plane Crazy* and *The Gallopin' Gaucho*. While Walt Disney originally voiced Minnie, he soon let Marcellite Garner, from the studio's Ink and Paint Department, take over.[11] Unlike Mickey's other co-stars, Minnie was beside Mickey from the very beginning.

Like her leading man, Mickey, Minnie went through several design changes throughout the decades. In the 1930s, she wore a small pillbox hat with a flower sticking out of it, and her eyes were two black olives with eyelids and lashes. From the beginning, she was connected with fashion, as her polka-dot skirt was inspired by the popular flapper fashion of that time period. In the 1940s, Minnie got her signature bow, which she has since rarely been seen without. Around the same time as Mickey's design was updated thanks to Fred Moore, similar changes were applied to Minnie, such as giving her a more pear-like shape and modifying her pupils. Two design traits that did remain were her signature heels, after her first animation in *Plane Crazy* in which she had no shoes, of course, and her eyelashes.

Currently, Minnie stars in the preschool television series *Mickey and the Roadster Racers* and appears in a variety of episodes of the Mickey Mouse shorts. As a style icon, she has inspired fashion runway shows around the world, has been dressed by the top fashion designers and has participated in countless fashion collaborations. To celebrate her popularity, Minnie received a Hollywood Walk of Fame star in 2018.

KEY TO PLATE

1: **Steamboat Willie**
1928
In this scene from *Steamboat Willie*, Mickey and Minnie see each other for the first time on screen. Minnie is calling from the shoreline to the boat. Mickey extends the crane, seen beside him in this image, out to Minnie to grab onto and be brought aboard.

2: **Steamboat Willie**
1928
In this scene from *Steamboat Willie*, Minnie makes her debut. Minnie is carrying her musical instrument and bag as she runs towards the boat in *Steamboat Willie*.

3: **Minnie in The Pet Store**
1933
In this scene from Minnie in *The Pet Store*, released October 28, 1933, Minnie has just entered the pet store and greeted Mickey. Shortly after, she is captured by a gigantic gorilla, who is imitating King Kong. Six months prior to the release of *The Pet Store*, the original *King Kong* premiered on 7 April, 1933.

4: ***Early model sheet of Minnie Mouse in a variety of action poses***
Her design includes pie-eyes, which were used in the early 1930s to suggest a reflection in the eye.

1

2
3

MINNIE MOUSE
53
4

DONALD DUCK

Donald Duck had a rather unusual beginning for an animated character. Typically, characters were developed on paper and then a voice was cast to bring personality to the character. Donald, on the other hand, was inspired by a voice and then the character was designed. The voice for Donald came from Clarence Nash, a radio performer, who instantly impressed Walt with his signature impressions. Disney needed a foil for Mickey who could provide comic relief and even get into a little bit of trouble now and again.

Donald's first appearance came in a *Silly Symphony* called *The Wise Little Hen* on 9 June, 1934. Drawing inspiration from the fairytale *The Little Red Hen*, a hen asks Peter Pig and Donald Duck to help her with some of the tasks associated with harvesting her corn. Both Peter and Donald deny each request, claiming they have stomach aches. Once she finishes harvesting her corn, she prepares a feast and asks one final request of Peter and Donald: Will they help her eat the corn? The pig and Donald's stomach aches suddenly vanish. The hen hands over a dish, but when they pull back the blanket they reveal a remedy for belly aches rather than the corn they were hoping for.

Donald's next appearance was two months later in *Orphans' Benefit* alongside Mickey Mouse. Mickey introduces Donald Duck to the audience and Donald recites "Mary Had a Little Lamb". He then performs "Little Boy Blue", but the orphans all blow their noses and Donald gets so angry he is escorted off stage.

Donald's first starring role was in *Donald and Pluto* released September 12, 1936. Donald would go on to appear in over 120 cartoons. In the 1940s, Donald even surpassed Mickey in popularity, becoming the most popular animated character in the world. One of Donald's most significant contributions has been his appearance in comics. Beginning on 7 February, 1938, a Donald Duck daily newspaper comic strip helped to further familiarise audiences with the irascible character. But one of his biggest moments came in 1942 when Carl Barks, a member of the Disney Story Department, started creating Donald Duck comic books with *Donald Duck Finds Pirate Gold.*

KEY TO PLATE

1: **Wise Little Hen, The**
1934
Donald Duck model sheet for *The Wise Little Hen* released June 9, 1934. In Donald's first appearance, the entrance of his waterfront dwelling is decorated with a ring buoy that ties into his sailor outfit.

2: **Orphans' Benefit**
1934
In this scene from *Orphans' Benefit*, released 11 August, 1934, Donald appears for the first time in a Mickey Mouse cartoon. Although Donald appears smaller than Mickey, his size would be adjusted in future animations. The short was remade (converted to colour with some new animation added) and released 12 August, 1941.

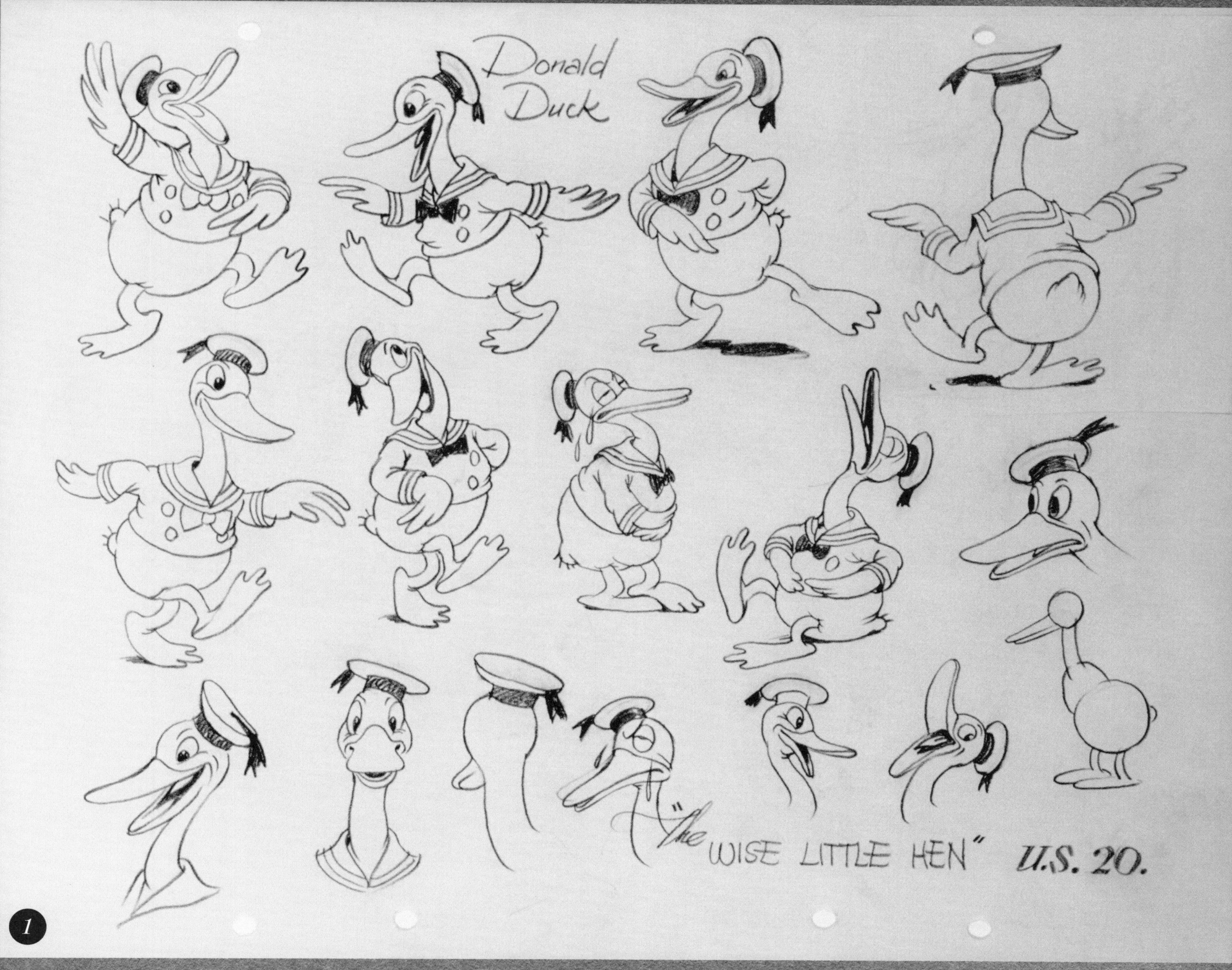

1

2

DAISY DUCK

Daisy Duck, Minnie Mouse's best friend, first made her appearance in *Don Donald* in 1937 as the romantic interest of Donald Duck. In this first appearance, her name is Donna Duck, as seen on a sign outside her property. In the short, Donald calls upon Donna and the two quickly get into an argument in which Donna shows she is a fair match for Donald's feistiness. Donald purchases a car to impress her, but the car seems to have a mind of its own. The car eventually ejects Donald and drives off with Donna, echoing a similar setup from *Plane Crazy*.

Three years later, the character's name is changed to Daisy Duck for *Mr. Duck Steps Out* which also starred Donald's nephews Huey, Dewey and Louie. When his nephews want to tag along on a visit to Daisy's house, Donald tries unsuccessfully to keep them at home. The nephews ultimately join him and, despite Donald's best efforts, they manage to get into quite a bit of mischief. Eventually, they cause Donald to swallow a piece of corn, ready to turn into popcorn, and he performs an inspired dance with Daisy.

Throughout the years, Daisy went through a variety of colour palettes in her wardrobe, though her design tended to remain similar. She was typically seen with a hair bow and similar heels to Minnie. In the 1950s, Daisy appeared in an entirely different fashion and had a more pronounced hairdo. Daisy continues to appear in Disney entertainment offerings to this day, including in Disney Channel television shows alongside her best friend, Minnie.

KEY TO PLATE

1: **Donald's Diary**
1954
Scene from *Donald's Diary* released 5 March, 1954. In animation from the 1950s as seen here, Daisy appeared in a variety of outfits and hairstyles that were a significant departure from her looks in previous decades.

2: **Donald's Double Trouble**
28 June, 1946
When Daisy breaks up with Donald, he encounters a duck who is identical to him, only this one speaks proper English and has manners. In this scene, it is the double, not Donald, who greets Daisy with flowers.

3: **Donald's Dilemma**
1947
In *Donald's Dilemma* released July 11, 1947, Daisy appears in a rare starring role. She recounts to a doctor about an incident where due to a head injury caused by a flower pot, Donald is able to sing beautifully, but he is cold to Daisy, as seen in this scene in which he refuses to shake her hand. Donald becomes famous and continues to ignore Daisy until she drops another pot on his head, returning Donald to his normal self.

GOOFY

Goofy's first appearance was in 1932 as an audience member in *Mickey's Revue*; though at the time he was unnamed. In 1933, he appeared in the Mickey Mouse newspaper comic strip as Dippy Dawg. Although he has been through several design changes (and monikers) since his debut, one signature mark never wavered: his iconic laugh originally provided by Pinto Colvig.

Since the beginning, Goofy was associated with Mickey and Donald. First appearing as a trio in 1935 in *Mickey's Service Station* the three friends play car repairmen who dismantle Peg Leg Pete's car as they attempt to locate the source of a noise that turns out to be a cricket. With no time to lose, they reassemble the car, but are not successful. Luckily, the car engine chases a grumpy Peg Leg Pete away.

As their relationships continued to evolve, Goofy and Donald typically provided the humour while Mickey was more serious, leaving the comedic opportunities to his co-stars. This dynamic led to Donald and Goofy eventually embarking on their own comedic duo adventure in the 1938 short *Polar Trappers*.

In the 1940s, Goofy appeared in a variety of how-to shorts in which he comically learns a sport or skill, such as how to swim. The next decade, Goofy went by the name George Geef, encountered more domesticated scenarios, and at times lost his signature droopy ears and some of his more goofy characteristics.

For all of his humorous adventures, two Goofy shorts did receive Academy Award® recognition with nominations for both *How to Play Football* (1944) and *Aquamania* (1961). Goofy continues to appear in animated shorts and comics, and will carry on his goofy antics for years to come.

1

2

KEY TO PLATE

1: **Whoopee Party, The**
1932
Promotional poster for *The Whoopee Party* released September 1932. Goofy takes on a more youthful appearance in this short than his first appearance several months earlier.

2: **Mickey's Revue**
1932
Promotional poster for *Mickey's Revue* released May 1932. In this short, Goofy makes his debut appearance as an audience member whose laugh bothers the characters seated near him. Though he is unnamed in the short, he would go on to be known as Dippy Dawg in the comics. In his debut, Goofy appeared older, with a white beard and square glasses.

3: **Goofy and Wilbur**
1939
Promotional poster for *Goofy and Wilbur* released March 1939. Goofy's first solo performance features Wilbur, a cricket who lures fish to Goofy's boat for him to catch.

WALT DISNEY'S
GOOFY and WILBUR
A "MICKEY MOUSE"

HOW TO FISH

© W.D.P.

R.K.O. RADIO PICTURE in TECHNICOLOR

Country of Origin U. S. A.

MORGAN LITHO. CORP. CLEVELAND, O.

14975

PLUTO

When Pluto first made his debut, it was actually in duplicate. He made a double appearance as an unnamed character in *The Chain Gang* in a minor role. One month later, he made his next appearance in *The Picnic* released 23 October, 1930. In this short, Pluto was named Rover and belonged not to Mickey, but Minnie, although Pluto does come bounding out of his doghouse and greets Mickey with enthusiastic kisses. Finally, in *The Moose Hunt* released 8 May, 1931, Pluto got his name and became Mickey's dog.

His first starring role came in 1937 with *Pluto's Quin-Puplets* in which he tries to keep track of his five rambunctious pups. Over his career, Pluto starred in 48 cartoons, with *Lend a Paw* winning an Academy Award® in the Best Short Subject Cartoon category in 1942.

Pluto began appearing in comics as early as 1931. Typically, comic books were reprinted material from the newspaper strips, but in 1942 in a comic book called *Pluto Saves the Ship* co-written by Carl Barks, original material was used for the first time. He also appeared on over 45 military insignias created by the Disney studio during the war. His image was one of the most requested, next in popularity to Donald Duck.

What makes Pluto different from Mickey's friends is he is a dog, not a human-like animal. Although he is mostly silent with the exception of *The Moose Hunt, Mickey's Kangaroo,* and *Pluto's Blue Note*, Pluto's voice was performed by Pinto Colvig, who was also the original voice of Goofy. Pluto is currently voiced by Bill Farmer, who is also the current voice of Goofy.

KEY TO PLATE

1: **Lend a Paw**
1941
Promotional poster for *Lend a Paw* released 3 October, 1941. This remake of *Mickey's Pal Pluto* (1933) won an Academy Award® in 1942.

2: **Pluto and the Gopher**
1950
Promotional poster for *Pluto and the Gopher* released 10 February, 1950. As seen in this short, Pluto's character design remains consistent throughout each decade.

3: **Moose Hunt, The**
1931
Promotional poster for *The Moose Hunt* released 8 May, 1931. In this short, Pluto accompanies Mickey on a hunting trip. In one of the rare times Pluto speaks, he says "kiss me" to Mickey.

1

2

3

COLUMBIA
PICTURES
presents

MICKEY MOUSE

in

THE MOOSE HUNT

Produced by WALT DISNEY

MORGAN LITHO CO.   This Poster is the Property of Columbia Pictures Corporation, and it is leased, not sold   M 8210   Made in U. S. A.

MORE FRIENDS AND SOME VILLAINS

If anyone is Mickey's main rival, it is Peg Leg Pete. Pete has actually been around longer than Mickey! In 1925, his debut came during the *Alice Comedies* where he was known by various names, including Bootleg Pete. He has been around since Mickey's debut in *Steamboat Willie* and he was also the first character to share the screen with Mickey. He has gone by a variety of names through the years – Pete, Bootleg Pete, Black Pete – but one thing has remained the same: this oversized character has given Mickey a rival to end all rivalries.

Mortimer Mouse, Mickey's original moniker, did turn into a character of his own; although he is a rat-like foil and nothing like Mickey. The name Mortimer appears early on in the daily newspaper comic strip.[12] Taken over by Floyd Gottfredson in April 1930, Minnie learns she has inherited "the old Mortimer mansion" in a strip called "Mickey Mouse in Death Valley" from 1 April, 1930. A few months later in September 1930, Mortimer made his first appearance in the comic strip. His first appearance on screen came in the Mickey Mouse short *Mickey's Rival* released 20 June, 1936, not as Uncle Mortimer but as a suitor trying to take Minnie's affection away from Mickey. Mortimer continues to appear in Mickey shorts to this day.

As for some of Mickey's other friends, Horace Horsecollar and Clarabelle Cow first met Mickey in a 1929 cartoon called *The Plowboy*. Not as often employed as Mickey's other co-stars, Horace Horsecollar appeared in 11 Mickey shorts while Clarabelle Cow has appeared in slightly more at 17; although some appearances were not Mickey shorts. Clarabelle Cow made her first appearance in the daily comic strip on 2 April, 1930 as a town gossip. The next day, Horace Horsecollar appeared in the strip having a chat with Mickey and Minnie. Both of these characters also occasionally appear on the Disney Channel television show *Mickey and the Roadster Racers*.

KEY TO PLATE

1: **Steamboat Willie**
1928
In this scene, Peg Leg Pete makes his debut with Mickey Mouse in *Steamboat Willie* 18 November, 1928. He was the first character to appear on screen with Mickey.

2: **Orphans' Benefit**
1934
Clarabelle Cow and Horace Horsecollar in *Orphans' Benefit* released 11 August, 1934. In this scene, Horace and Clarabelle are performing with Goofy following Donald Duck's performance.

3: **Mickey's Rival**
1936
In this scene from *Mickey's Rival* released June 20, 1936, Minnie introduces Mickey to Mortimer by saying, "Mickey, I want you to meet Mortimer. He's a perfect scream." Mickey and Minnie are settling down to a picnic when Mortimer races by, disrupting their preparations. Mortimer is a prankster, and each prank upsets Mickey more until an angry bull happens upon the picnic and Mickey needs to save the day.

JOSEPH M. SCHENCK Presents WALT DISNEY'S
Mickey Mouse in "THE ORPHANS' BENEFIT"

SECTION 4

MICKEY MERCHANDISING

In the Beginning
Mickey Books
Mickey the Comic
Stamps

IN THE BEGINNING

In September 1929, Harry Woodin, the manager of the Fox Dome Theater in Ocean Park, California, saw a major opportunity to bring children together for activities with Mickey Mouse. Every Saturday, the Mickey Mouse Club was a place where children could go to enjoy their favourite character, and parents could get a break. Attendees would recite the Mickey Mouse creed written by Harry Woodin that stated "Mickey Mice do not swear, smoke, cheat, or lie". There were songs, games and, of course, Mickey Mouse screenings. There was even an "Official Bulletin for the Mickey Mouse Club", which would contain announcements about new Mickey Mouse Club chapters, information on merchandise and other general club occurrences.

Originally conceived by Woodin, he extended an invitation to Walt to come and see it for himself. With Walt's approval, Harry expanded the club to other movie theatres. By October 1932, the Mickey Mouse Club was one million members strong with merchants selling Mickey Mouse products outside of each gathering. Three years later, there were over 700 chapters across the United States.[13]

As far as the merchandise being sold outside of the theatres, Walt had made several licensing deals. On 29 January, 1930, George Borgfeldt & Company signed a deal to

make Mickey and Minnie toys.[14] Also during 1930, Charlotte Clark began making stuffed Mickey and Minnie dolls in two sizes: 16 to 18 inches and 3 feet tall.[15]

Realising the potential of licensing, Walt signed on Kay Kamen as a licensing agent for Disney in 1932. Kay Kamen immediately got to work, signing hundreds of deals and putting Mickey's image all over department stores. The first Mickey Mouse wristwatches by the Ingersoll-Waterbury Clock Company were produced by summer 1933. In May 1934, Lionel Train corporation produced a Mickey and Minnie toy handcar. Over 250,000 orders came in by the end of the year, saving the company from going out of business.[16]

On 10 March, 1935, a *New York Times* article titled "Mickey Mouse Emerges as Economist" stated: "Now there are eighty licensees in the United States, fifteen in Canada, forty in England, eighty on the Continent and fifteen in Australia.[17] There are branch offices in Chicago, Toronto, London, Paris, Copenhagen, Milan, Barcelona, Lisbon and Sydney." By 1935, Mickey was an international merchandising hit.

KEY TO PLATE

***1:* Mickey Mouse Club**
circa 1930
Button from the early Mickey Mouse Clubs.

***2:* Original Charlotte Clark Mickey Mouse doll**
circa 1930
To ensure all children could afford a Mickey Mouse doll, Disney issued a Mickey and Minnie pattern available for purchase for 35 cents.

***3:* Mickey Mouse Club**
circa 1930
Mickey Mouse Club membership application.

MICKEY MOUSE CLUB

FOR BOYS AND GIRLS

A MESSAGE TO BOYS AND GIRLS
from the
Manager of This Theatre

Dear Little Friends:--

A short time ago I read, in one of the theatrical publications coming to my desk, something about the MICKEY MOUS CLUB for Boys and Girls. The article mentioned how much fun it meant for its members, how it helped them to be good little American citizens, and rewarded them for good behavior in the home, good work in the school and good sportsmanship on the playground.

Believing no community in the United States has finer boys and girls than ours, I, naturally, was interested and from Mickey Mouseville at the Disney Studios in Hollywood, Calif., I obtained all information. I wish I had the space here to pass what I learned on to you—but this is out of the question so all I can tell you here is to take my word for it that you're going to be ever so happy that we're going to have a MICKEY MOUSE CLUB in this community.

I cannot urge you too strongly to lose no time in securing and filling out a Membership Application Blank, for this will not only bring you special consideration at the first matinee, (See Page 1 for Special Offer) but will entitle you to Official Membership Card and Button, which, in turn, will mean participation in lots of good times and other privileges and benefits.

Trusting to number you among my MICKEY MOUSE CLUB pals,

THE MANAGER.

MICKEY MOUSE CLUB

MICKEY MOUSE CLUB

FOR BOYS AND GIRLS

HERE IS THE OFFICIAL MICKEY MOUSE CLUB MEMBERSHIP CARD

MEMBER MICKEY MOUSE CLUB
__________ Theatre
This Certifies that __________
is a Registered Member of the
MICKEY MOUSE CLUB
See Reverse Side
Chief Mickey Mouse

AND HERE IS THE OFFICIAL MICKEY MOUSE BUTTON

MICKEY MOUSE CLUB

Membership Card and Button, illustrated at left, will be given Boys and Girls FREE upon presentation of Membership Application Forms properly filled out. Application Blanks can be obtained FREE from OFFICIAL MICKEY MOUSE STORES listed on Back Page. Get Your Membership Card and Button, Boys and Girls —They're Going to be Valuable and Helpful in Many Ways. Surprises Prize Offers, Special Rewards and Many Other Attractive Events are Being Arranged for Members in Good Standing and a Member in Good Standing is a Boy or Girl who Secures and Carries a Membership Card and Wears the Mickey Mouse Club Button at all times.

MICKEY MOUSE CLUB CREED

I will be a square shooter in my home, in school, on the playgrounds, where-ever I may be.
I will be truthful and honorable and strive, always, to make myself a better and more useful little citizen.
I will respect my elders and help the aged, the helpless and children smaller than myself.
In short, I will be a good American!—

MICKEY MOUSE CLUB

3

MICKEY BOOKS

It is impossible to imagine a time when Mickey Mouse did not appear in comics and books, or on products like cups and T-shirts. The first licence for a Mickey Mouse product was in 1929 and it happened by a chance encounter while Walt was in New York. A man gave Walt 300 dollars to use Mickey's image on school writing tablets for children.[18]

The first Mickey Mouse book was published in 1930 by the New York-based publishers Bibo and Lang. It features an original story that tells the tale of Mickey's origins, in which he is "mouse number thirteen" from Mouse Fairyland. He is ejected from his home and lands "on a roof in Hollywood, California". The story then continues to reveal how Mickey and Walt met. This story is followed by a game called "The Mickey Mouse Journey", a comic where Mickey and Minnie encounter some owls, game pieces and sheet music for a Mickey Mouse song.

The first full-colour hardcover Mickey Mouse book was published in 1931 by the David McKay Company of Philadelphia.[19] It tells the story of Mickey Mouse "who lives in a cozy nest under the floor of the old barn" and his friend Minnie Mouse as they try to escape Claws, the Cat. Inside this book, the name Donald Duck appears; although Donald would not make his screen debut until three years later in *The Wise Little Hen*. On the first page, he is listed as one of Mickey's friends and he also appears on the back cover of the book.

The first *Mickey Mouse Magazine* was published in January 1933.

KEY TO PLATE

1: **Mickey Mouse Book**
Front cover of the first Mickey Mouse book. It features an original story, a game with game pieces, sheet music and a comic.

2: **The Adventures of Mickey Mouse *Book #1***
Back cover of *The Adventures of Mickey Mouse*, Book #1. An early illustration of Donald Duck can be seen on the lower left-hand corner of the image.

3: **The Adventures of Mickey Mouse *Book #2***
Front cover of *The Adventures of Mickey Mouse*, Book #2 featuring Mickey and Pluto on the cover.

4: **The Adventures of Mickey Mouse *Book #1***
Front cover of the first full-colour Mickey Mouse book, *The Adventures of Mickey Mouse*, published by the David McKay Company. The dedication from Walt reads: "Dedicated to Mickey's millions of friends thruout [sic] the world."

5: **The Adventures of Mickey Mouse *Book #1***
Interior spread from *The Adventures of Mickey Mouse* Book #1. In this book, the name Donald Duck appears for the first time in print as seen here.

There were Carolyn Cow, Donald Duck, Clara Cluck, the Hen, Patricia Pig, Robert Rooster, Long Dog, the Dachshund, George and Gertie Goat, and all of their families.

Then they went all around the barnyard ; to the pig-pen, the duck-pond and everywhere. Mickey asked all of his friends to come to the dance in the big room in the barn. They all said they would.

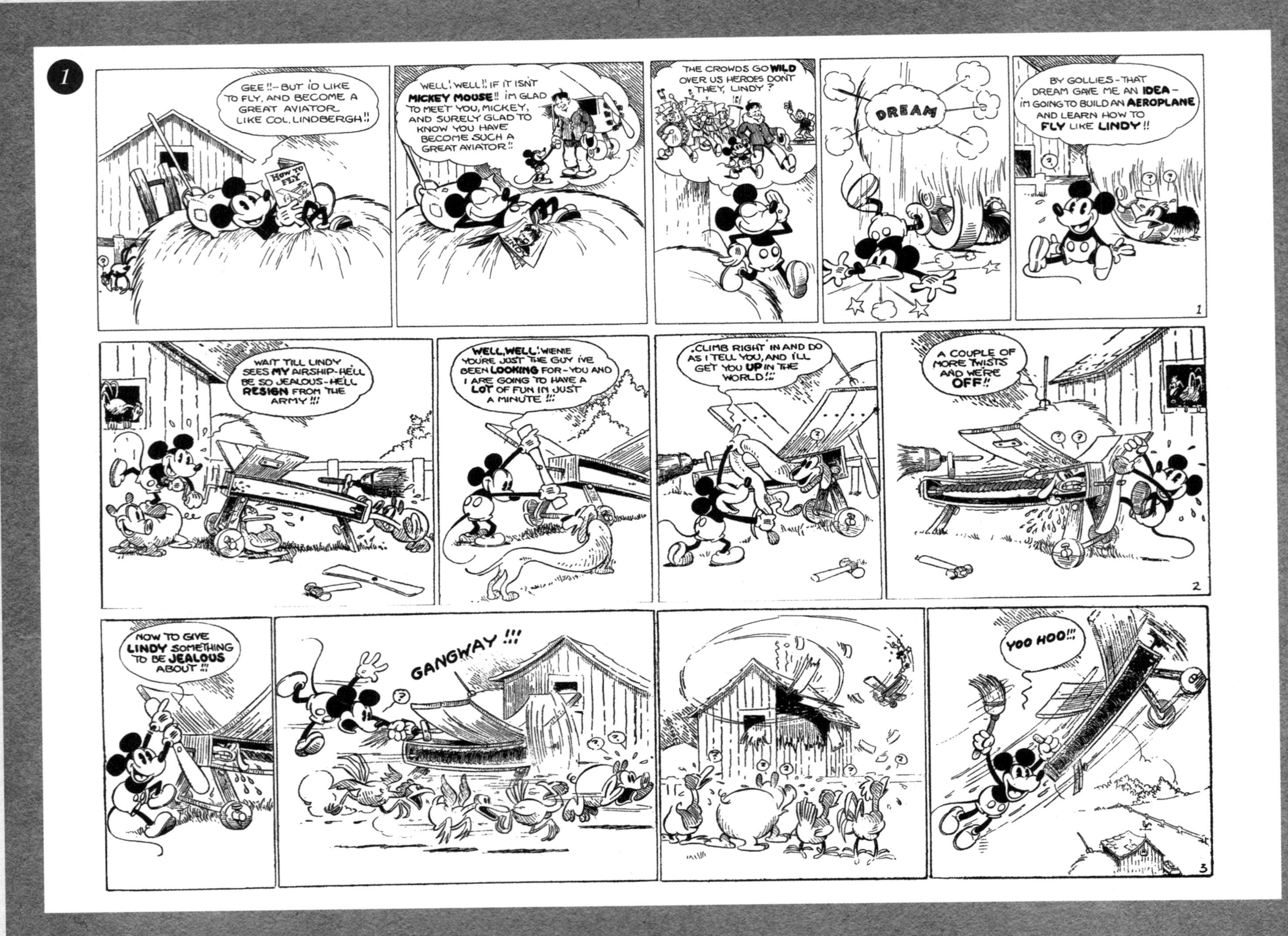

MICKEY THE COMIC

In order to secure Mickey as a global icon, Disney entered into comics early on in Mickey's career. Mickey's very own newspaper comic strip debuted Monday, 13 January, 1930. Originally, Walt wrote the comics and Ub Iwerks drew them. The first Mickey Mouse daily comic strip was inspired by the plot of *Plane Crazy;* it was common at the time for comics to incorporate plot lines from the shorts. The first character to appear with Mickey was, of course, Minnie Mouse. She made her first appearance on the sixth day of the comic.

As the studio was growing quickly and Walt's attention was needed elsewhere, on 5 May, 1930, Floyd Gottfredson, a former theatre projectionist, took over on what was initially a temporary basis. Floyd would eventually wear a variety of hats in the comics department over the next several decades, whether he wrote the comics, drew them or headed up the department. In a letter to David R. Smith, dated November 1975, Floyd writes: "During the continuities – this is the way Walt started [Mickey]

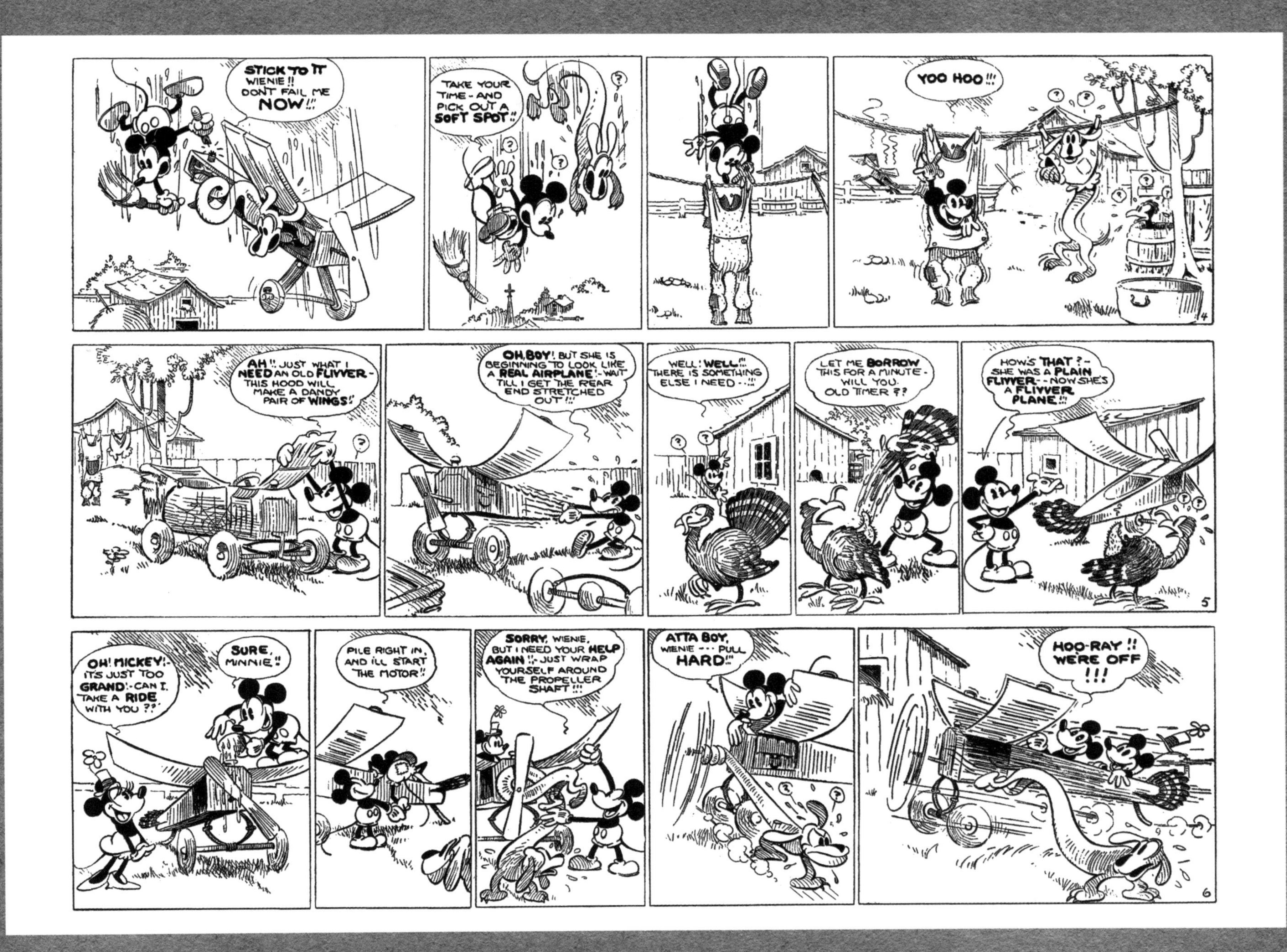

out in the continuity and it's the way I carried him on – he was a Mouse Against The World sort of character. Not that he was belligerent or militant, or really against the world – it was just that the world was so much bigger than him. He was constantly getting into scrapes and situations that he had to fumble his way out of – not as dangerous as Superman or anything – but in a funny sort of way. When he was in a corner, he was a feisty little guy who would fight his way out."[20] Floyd used the comics as an opportunity to expand Mickey's world, creating characters like the Phantom Blot and Eega Beeva. Gottfredson also added members of Mickey's family, including his nephews Morty and Ferdy Fieldmouse on 18 September, 1932.

In October 1930, the Mickey Mouse comic strip appeared in *Le Petit Parisien*, a French daily publication. Only a few short months later, Mickey's comic strip appeared in over 20 countries around the world in over 40 newspapers. Mickey appeared in his first international comic book in Italy with the publication of *Topolino* in 1932. By 1937, his comic strips would appear in 27 languages.[21]

KEY TO PLATE

***1:* Mickey Mouse comic book**
First six days of the Mickey Mouse comic strip. Written by Walt Disney, illustrated by Ub Iwerks, and inked by Win Smith. The story is similar to *Plane Crazy*, also written by Walt Disney and animated by Ub Iwerks.

STAMPS

From Grenada to Gambia, Mickey and his friends have appeared on postage stamps for over four decades. Mickey has appeared in a variety of situations, including celebrations for the International Year of the Child, the Olympics, Christmas and Easter. He has played several sports from soccer, tennis and scuba diving to fishing, pole vaulting and baseball. One of the most common themes across the decades has been Mickey stamps tied into a holiday theme. He has delivered letters as a mailman and collected stamps with Pluto. He has flown to outer space and gone sledding in Alaska. And all of those adventures happened in just the first two decades.

In the United States, it took until 1968 for the first Disney stamp to appear. It was a portrait of Walt, commemorating his contribution to the world. Issued 30 years later, Snow White was included in the "Celebrate the Century" collection, helping to represent the 1930s.

In 2003, Mickey's 75th anniversary, the United States Post Office (USPS) announced that Mickey Mouse and his friends would appear in a series of commemorative stamps. This was the first time Mickey would appear on a stamp in the US. That series eventually became the Art of Disney series, which according to a 2008 press release from the USPS, is "the most popular stamp series in US Postal Service history" with over 200 million stamps sold.[22] Mickey was the only character included in each set.

The first in the series was The Art of Disney Friendship (2004), which featured Mickey and his two best friends, Donald and Goofy. Next, The Art of Disney Celebration (2005) was released, including a stamp depicting Mickey and his pal Pluto with a cake. The following year, The Art of Disney Romance depicted Minnie kissing Mickey. In 2007, The Art of Disney Magic included Mickey in his look from *The Sorcerer's Apprentice*. This would be the first US stamp to depict Mickey alone. The final set in the series titled The Art of Disney Imagination (2008) depicts Mickey in his classic *Steamboat Willie* appearance. The text that accompanies this stamp reads: "Walt Disney once said that Mickey was 'created for the purpose of laughter.' From the moment Walt first imagined him, Mickey has been a happy reminder that a little laughter goes a long way; it's hard to imagine the world without his familiar smile."

KEY TO PLATE

***1:* First US postage stamp featuring Mickey**
2004
This stamp of Mickey was a part of The Art of Disney Friendship series.

***2:* Second US postage stamp featuring Mickey**
2005
The second US postage stamp of Mickey, released in 2005, was a part of The Art of Disney Celebration series.

***3:* US Postage Stamp**
2007
The first US postage stamp to feature Mickey alone was released in 2007. This stamp was part of The Art of Disney Magic series.

***4:* Sharjah postage stamp**
Postage stamp from Sharjah featuring Mickey and Donald climbing a mountain.

***5:* San Marino postage stamp**
circa 1970
Postage stamp from the Republic of San Marino *circa* December 1970.

37
USA

1

usa
2005

2

41
USA
2007

3

75DH
SHARJAH
& DEPENDENCIES
بريد جوي
AIR MAIL
الشارقة
وملحقاتها

4

WALT DISNEY
production
REP. SAN
MARINO
L. 90
I.P.S. - ROMA - 1970

5

SECTION 5

ANIMATED MICKEY

1929–1935 It's All Black-and-White
Design Magic
1935–1953 A Life in Colour
Fantasia
The Mickey Mouse Club TV Show
Mickey's Back

1929–1935 IT'S ALL BLACK-AND-WHITE

After the first three Mickey Mouse short films were released, Mickey continued to appear regularly in black-and-white animation. The fourth Mickey short to be produced was *The Barn Dance*. In this film, Mickey attends a dance with Minnie, where his heavy-footed moves cause Minnie some distress. Minnie selects a replacement dance partner, but Mickey comes up with a quick solution: to use a balloon to make his feet lighter.

The year 1929 continued to hold significant milestones for Mickey. Mickey's fifth film, *The Opry House,* was the first time Mickey donned his signature white gloves, which he wears while playing a lively piano for a packed audience. The piano eventually takes on a personality of its own, playing keys when the mood strikes and even ejecting Mickey from the stage. Mickey's appearance in *The Jazz Fool*, was the first time he was shown with pie-eyes, a common technique used in animation during that time to suggest a reflection in a character's eyes. In *The Karnival Kid,* Mickey plays the role of a hot dog vendor at a carnival. In this short, he says his first words on screen, which were: "Hot Dogs! Hot Dogs!" Mickey also gained two new friends in 1929 with the first appearances of Horace Horsecollar and Clarabelle Cow in *The Plowboy.*

During this time, music played a vital role in the cartoons, with Mickey sometimes playing the role of lead entertainer, dancing to music, playing music and even sometimes playing his body as an instrument, like in *Mickey's Follies* when he played his teeth like a xylophone. In *Mickey's Follies* audiences were introduced to the song "Minnie's Yoo Hoo" written by Carl Stalling. Mickey performs this song to an audience of animals at an outdoor concert. This song would go on the become the theme song of the original Mickey Mouse Clubs and became the first song Disney made available to the public as sheet music.

The early thirties also introduced audiences to the dog that would become known as Pluto, first in 1931's *The Moose Hunt* – the character that would later garner acclaim as Goofy in *Mickey's Revue* in 1932, and Donald Duck in *Orphans' Benefit* two years later in 1934. By Mickey's 7th birthday, a new era was on the horizon that would change the animated art form forever. *Mickey's Service Station*, released on 16 March, 1935, would be the final Mickey Mouse cartoon produced in black-and-white. It also established Donald, Goofy and Mickey as a comedic trio for the first time.[23]

KEY TO PLATE

***1:* Mickey's Orphans**
1931
Promotional poster for *Mickey's Orphans* released 9 December, 1931. This was the first Mickey Mouse short nominated for an Academy Award®. Walt Disney's *Flowers and Trees* took home the Oscar, but Disney did win a special Oscar for the creation of Mickey.

***2:* Musical Farmer**
1932
Promotional poster for *Musical Farmer* released 9 July, 1932. In this short, Mickey, Minnie and Pluto are working on a farm where all the activity takes on a musical quality, a common theme during this time period.

3: Promotional material
circa 1935
This image appeared in promotional material *circa* 1935. On the left is an early design of Mickey from 1928. On the right is Mickey as he appeared in 1935.

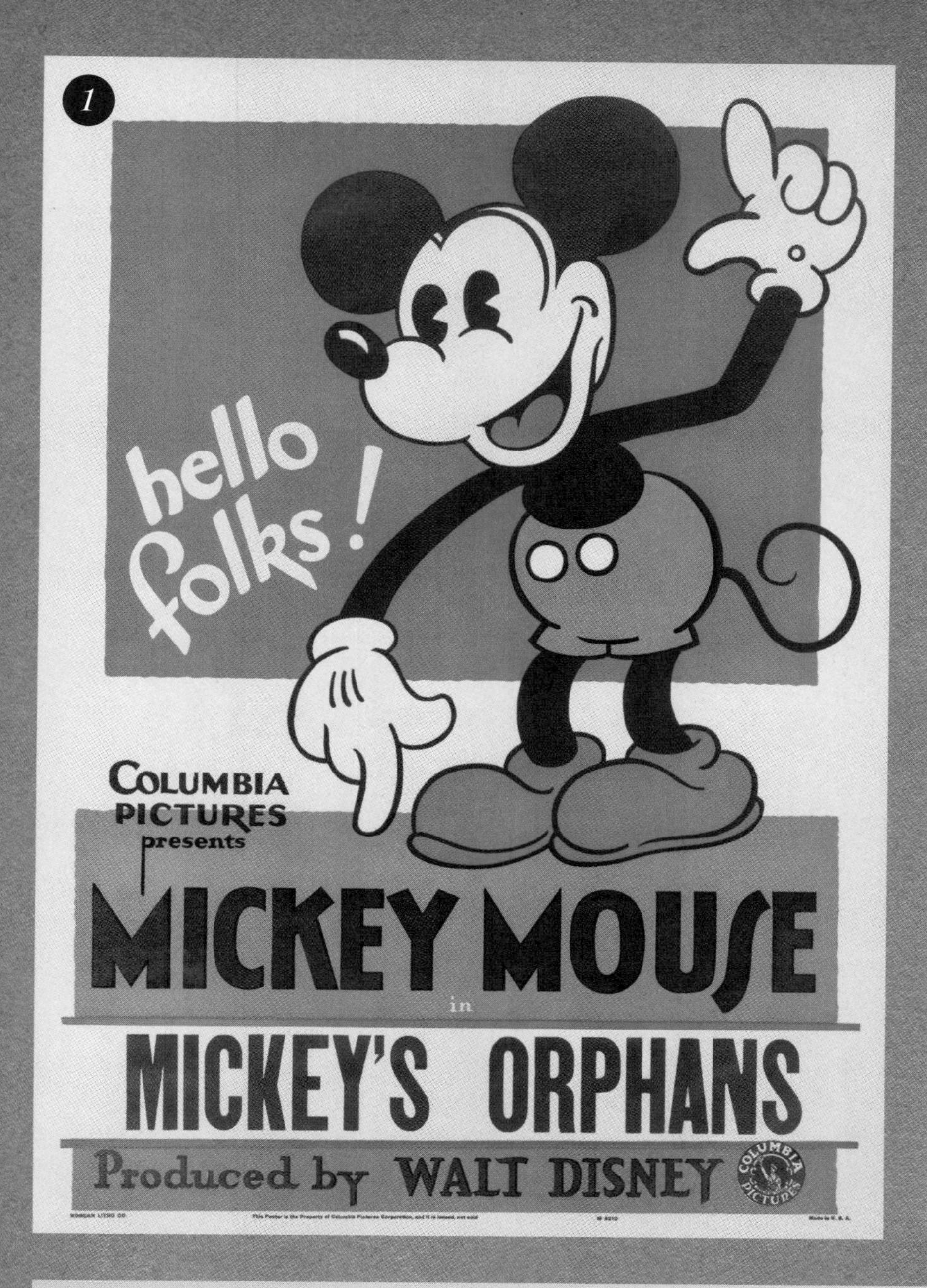
1
hello folks!
COLUMBIA PICTURES presents
MICKEY MOUSE
in
MICKEY'S ORPHANS
Produced by WALT DISNEY
COLUMBIA PICTURES

2
MICKEY MOUSE
IN
"THE MUSICAL FARMER"
Produced by WALT DISNEY
A COLUMBIA Picture

3
© W. D. P

1

DESIGN MAGIC

In Mickey's first short, *Plane Crazy*, he was shoeless and without gloves. He gained a pair of shoes in *Steamboat Willie*, but was still bare-handed. *The Opry House* was the first time Mickey donned a pair of his signature white gloves, which helped differentiate his hands from his arms. Of course, the glove only has room for three fingers and a thumb. He would go on to wear these gloves for the first time throughout an entire short in *When the Cat's Away*, after which they would become a mainstay of his wardrobe. In a 1949 article from Collier's titled "Mickey Mouse and How He Grew" by Irving Wallace, Disney said: "Artistically, five digits are too many for a mouse. His hand would look like a bunch of bananas. Financially, not having an extra finger in each of 45,000 drawings that make up a six and one-half minute short has saved the studio millions."[24] One thing that has remained the same in Mickey's design is his circular black ears. They are his signature feature and recognised as his symbol internationally.

Some of the most impactful design changes were made to Mickey in the late 1930s and early 1940s, when Fred Moore was tasked with redesigning the character. One model sheet from that time period has notes that read: "notice how black part of head alters as Mickey changes expressions" and "make nose definitely stick out from head".[25]

Mickey's new design featured a pear-shaped body, distinct pupils and eyebrows.

Following Mickey turning half a century in age, a Harvard professor named Stephen Jay Gould published an article in *Natural History's* May 1979 issue titled "Mickey Mouse Meets Konrad Lorenz". The first argument he presented involved Mickey's personality from his inception to 50 years later. Gould pointed out that Mickey used to be much more rambunctious and full of mischief. The character Mickey Mouse had grown up to be much better behaved. In conjunction with this behaviour shift, Mickey's appearance changed as well.

His second argument was that Mickey experienced three major changes in appearance during his first 50 years: increase in eye size, increase in head size compared to body and a thinner nose with ears forwards. Those changes in appearance, Gould concluded, could be compared to those of a human baby. Citing an article by Konrad Lorenz, Gould argues that "features of juvenility trigger 'innate releasing mechanisms' for affection and nurturance in adult humans". And the same concept can be applied to the changing features of Mickey Mouse. Gould ultimately concluded that the Disney animators did not intentionally shift Mickey towards a cuter aesthetic.

KEY TO PLATE

1: Mickey Mouse Meets Konrad Lorenz

This image accompanied Gould's 1979 article "Mickey Mouse Meets Konrad Lorenz". The first two images of Mickey on the left are how he appeared in the 1930s. The three Mickeys in the middle appeared during the 1940s and the Mickey on the far right appeared in the 1970s.

1935–1953 A LIFE IN COLOUR

Perhaps the second monumental shift for Mickey Mouse came in early 1935, when he appeared in his first theatrically released colour film, *The Band Concert*. Mickey, playing the role of conductor, wears yellow shoes, a red conductor outfit with green trim, and yellow buttons and tassels. The short made such an impression that writer Gilbert Seldes in *Esquire* magazine called it, "Disney's greatest single work."

This was not Mickey's first appearance in colour, however. His multichromatic debut came three years prior, when he appeared in a short created for the Academy Awards® called *Parade of the Award Nominees* in November 1932. This was the year in which Disney received a special Academy Award® for the creation of Mickey Mouse and *Flowers and Trees* won an Oscar.[26] In 1939, Mickey would return to the Oscars with his nomination for *Brave Little Tailor* (1938), only to lose out to a different Disney film, *Ferdinand the Bull.*

Just as *Plane Crazy* and *The Gallopin' Gaucho* were converted to synchronised sound films with the advancement of technology, a few of Mickey's black-and-white films were converted to colour such as *Orphans' Benefit*. A few shorts in the 1940s like *The Little Whirlwind* showed Mickey and Minnie with teeth. The beginning of the 1940s also saw the debut of Mickey's signature red shorts in films like *Mr. Mouse Takes a Trip.*

In 1939's *The Pointer*, Mickey appeared in a newly designed way thanks to Fred Moore's work. Mickey had more of a pear-like body shape, a more childlike appearance, and eyes with distinct pupils. This short was nominated for an Academy Award® as well.

In 1953, Mickey made his final appearance in the last regular instalment of the Mickey Mouse classic shorts in *The Simple Things*. In the final scene, Mickey and Pluto run away from a flock of aggressive seagulls. Mickey would not return to the screen for another 30 years.

KEY TO PLATE

***1:* The Band Concert**
1935
Animation cel setup from Mickey's first colour short, *The Band Concert* released 23 February, 1935. Mickey is conducting the "William Tell Overture", when the performance is quickly interrupted by Donald Duck, the only character with a speaking part. A tornado appears in the distance, slowly making its way towards the concert and consuming everything in its path. Soon, the band is taken up in the whirlwind as Mickey continues to conduct the orchestra. The orchestra settles back down to earth and finishes the piece.

***2:* The Pointer**
1939
Promotional poster for *The Pointer* released 21 July, 1939. In *The Pointer,* Mickey and Pluto go on a hunting excursion. When Pluto's instincts get ahead of him, Mickey needs to teach Pluto how to be a pointer. Then, Mickey accidentally awakens a large bear, mistaking him for Pluto. Mickey comes across Pluto and realises his mistake. Mickey tries to reason with the enraged bear to the best of his ability and ultimately escapes.

***3:* The Simple Things**
1953
Promotional poster for *The Simple Things* released 18 April, 1953. In this short, Mickey goes on a fishing excursion with his pal Pluto. While they are fishing, a seagull begins to pester Mickey and Pluto. Eventually, a flock of seagulls descends on them and chases them off the beach.

Walt Disney's
MICKEY MOUSE
presents
THE POINTER
in TECHNICOLOR
© W.D.P.
When you see "The Pointer" announced for showing at your favorite movie you'll know you're in for a real laugh treat! .. A'hunting they go—and what happens will keep you in stitches! .. Don't miss it, no matter what else is on the program.
DISTRIBUTED BY RKO RADIO PICTURES

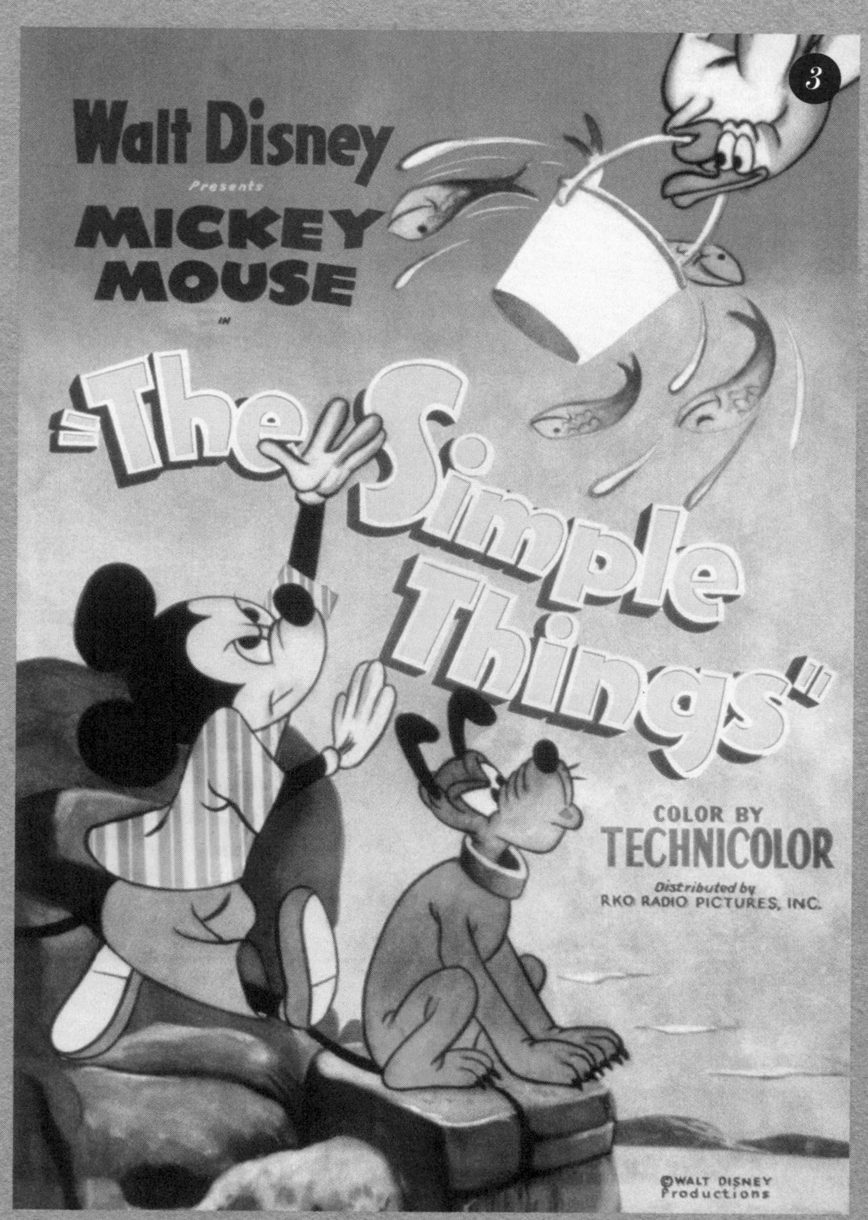
Walt Disney
Presents
MICKEY
MOUSE
"The Simple Things"
COLOR BY
TECHNICOLOR
Distributed by
RKO RADIO PICTURES, INC.
©WALT DISNEY
Productions

FANTASIA

In 1937, Disney began production on a *Silly Symphony* titled *The Sorcerer's Apprentice*. However, several factors, including, a chance encounter in Los Angeles, between Walt Disney and conductor Leopold Stokowski, would lead to the short being included in the feature film *Fantasia*.The full-length feature would include eight shorts accompanied by music conducted by Stokowski. *The Sorcerer's Apprentice* remained the centrepiece of the expanded feature film.

For the theatrical release of *Fantasia*, Walt developed a special sound system called Fantasound, which used multiple speakers placed throughout the theatre. This made it seem as though the orchestra was playing live during the screening. Prior to *Fantasia*, the sound in the theatre typically came only from the front of the auditorium. One of the two Academy Awards® *Fantasia* received recognised the importance of Fantasound.

Fantasia premiered in New York City on 13 November, 1940 at the same theatre where *Steamboat Willie* first premiered 12 years prior almost exactly to the date.

Following its initial release, *Fantasia* was rereleased in theatres eight times. Walt's vision of *Fantasia* being a recurring theatrical event with new segments added each year was finally realised 60 years after the original release with *Fantasia/2000*. This feature included eight new sequences, keeping only *The Sorcerer's Apprentice* from the original movie.

KEY TO PLATE

1: **The Sorcerer's Apprentice**
1940
Concept art for *The Sorcerer's Apprentice*. This scene occurs immediately after Yensid leaves his sorcerer's hat behind. Following this image, Mickey runs towards the hat and places it atop his head.

2: **The Sorcerer's Apprentice**
1940
In a dreamlike state, Mickey takes command of the stars shortly after falling asleep in a segment that has become iconic to the film.

3: **The Sorcerer's Apprentice**
1940
Concept art for *The Sorcerer's Apprentice*. Fred Moore was tasked with updating Mickey's design around the time work on *Fantasia* commenced in 1937. His redesign featured pupils in Mickey's eyes, a pear-shaped body and eyebrows, which would be used in *Fantasia*.

4: **The Sorcerer's Apprentice**
1940
Concept art for *The Sorcerer's Apprentice*. In his first full-length feature, Mickey Mouse wears his signature sorcerer's hat, which has become an important symbol for Mickey and The Walt Disney Company.

5: **Fantasia**
1940
Original release poster for *Fantasia*. At first, *Fantasia* was referred to as *The Concert Feature*.[27] Disney held a naming contest, with approximately 1800 titles being submitted by over 250 employees. They ultimately decided to go with an early working title, *Fantasia*.

5

THE MICKEY MOUSE CLUB TV SHOW

Three months after the opening of Disneyland, the Mickey Mouse Club television show premiered on 3 October, 1955. It was conceived of as an hour-long daily programme composed of segments, including news, cartoons, music and talent shows featuring a cast of children called Mouseketeers, nine of whom would perform on all four years of the show. Each day of the week had a special theme, ranging from "Fun with Music Day" to "Talent Roundup Day." The show was an instant success, with 10 million viewers every episode of the first season.[28]

One of the most iconic features of the Mickey Mouse Club were Mickey ears worn by the Mouseketeers. In an interview with NPR, Annette Funicello said about those ears: "Well it was a shock because I think the first thing we thought – especially the boys – was, what do you mean I have to wear those things on my head?"[29] Within the first three months of the show's premiere, Disney would sell two million of "those things".[30]

Another iconic feature to come out of the original Mickey Mouse Club was the theme song, the "Mickey Mouse March". The lyrics famously go: "Who's the leader of the club that's made for you and me? M-I-C-K-E-Y M-O-U-S-E!" This song was written by Jimmie Dodd, who was also the master of ceremonies on the show. The original Mickey Mouse Club ended on 25 September, 1959.

The Mickey Mouse Club was back on the air several times throughout the decades. In 1977, a "new" Mickey Mouse Club premiered featuring 12 new Mouseketeers. This series lasted until 1 December, 1978. In the 1990s, the Mickey Mouse Club was revived yet again. The third version of this series would feature Britney Spears, Justin Timberlake, Ryan Gosling and Christina Aguilera. This series exchanged the Mickey Mouse ear hats for letterman-style jackets. It was filmed in front of a live studio audience, which was a first for the series.

On 8 September, 2017, a whole new set of Mouseketeers graced the screen, only this time the screen they would appear on would be digital screens. Existing entirely through social media, Club Mickey Mouse is ready to entertain the next generation of fans.

KEY TO PLATE

1: ***Photograh of Jimmie Dodd and Roy Williams***
Roy Williams was the other adult co-host of the Mickey Mouse Club. It was his idea to get the Mouseketeers to wear Mickey Mouse ear hats.[31]

2: ***Mickey Mouse Club***
The original logo for the Mickey Mouse Club.

MICKEY'S BACK

In 1983, Mickey would make his triumphant return to the silver screen in *Mickey's Christmas Carol*. Mickey and his friends were cast in the roles of the Charles Dickens' classic, *A Christmas Carol*. This was the final performance by Clarence Nash for Donald Duck's voice. It premiered first in the UK on 20 October, 1983, then in the US on 16 December, 1983. It received an Academy Award® nomination for Best Animated Short Film. The film was actually inspired by a musical album from 1974, in which Mickey and his friends play the roles from *A Christmas Carol*. The album script was adapted for the script of the animated cartoon.

The Prince and the Pauper was another Mickey film inspired by classic literature, released on 16 November, 1990. In Janet Maslin's review of the film in *The New York Times*, she states: "Savvy enough to keep its bigger viewers at least marginally interested, it should also charm young audiences with its nimble animation and frequent, well-staged gags.[32] As directed by George Scribner, who did *Oliver & Company*, this short feature has energy and dash. Mickey himself, with the new and slightly squeakier voice of Wayne Allwine, is in good company and good form."

On 1 May, 1999, *Mickey MouseWorks* premiered on Saturday morning on ABC. In an interview with the *Los Angeles Times*, co-executive producer Tony Craig said, "We went back to Walt's theories about Mickey being the little guy, the underdog who comes out a winner, just because he tries really hard and has determination and spirit [...] For the look of the character, we drew our inspiration from the Mickey animated by Fred Moore, Ward Kimball and Walt Kelly in 1941 in *The Nifty Nineties* and *The Little Whirlwind*. It's basically that version of the design, with slightly larger hands and feet and a more streamlined body."[33]

Following this series, on 13 January, 2001 *House of Mouse* premiered on ABC and would have a total of 52 episodes. But with advancements in computer-generated animation, the industry was about to transform, and so too would Mickey.

KEY TO PLATE

1: **Mickey's Christmas Carol**
1983
In *Mickey's Christmas Carol*, released 16 December, 1983, Mickey Mouse plays Bob Cratchit with Minnie Mouse as Mrs Cratchit. Melody, Ferdy and Morty play Bob Cratchit's children, with Morty playing Tiny Tim. Ebenezer Scrooge is, of course, played by Scrooge McDuck.

2: **The Ghost of Christmas Past**
Scene from *Mickey's Christmas Carol*, in which the role of the Ghost of Christmas Past is played by Jiminy Cricket.

3: **Mickey as Bob Cratchit**
Scene from *Mickey's Christmas Carol*. Mickey's voice was performed by Wayne Allwine.

4: **The Ghost of Christmas Present**
Scene from *Mickey's Christmas Carol*, in which the role of the Ghost of Christmas Present is played by Willie the Giant. Willie made his debut in 1947 with the release of *Mickey and the Beanstalk*.

5: **The Ghost of Christmas Future**
Scene from *Mickey's Christmas Carol* in which the role of the Ghost of Christmas Future is played by a masked figure who eventually reveals himself to be Pete.

6: **Ebenezer Scrooge**
Final scene from *Mickey's Christmas Carol*, in which Ebenezer Scrooge, played by Scrooge McDuck, has shown generosity to the Cratchit family and is embraced by them.

BLESS
OUR
1

2

3

4

R.I.P.
EBENEZER
SCROOGE
5

6

SECTION 6

MICKEY AT LARGE

Disneyland
Hollywood Legend
International Star
Mickey at War

DISNEYLAND

Disneyland opened on 17 July, 1955 in Anaheim, California, within just one year of initial construction beginning. Cousins Christine Vess, five years old, and Michael Schwartner, seven years old, were the first guests. When Disneyland originally opened there were 20 attractions, including Jungle Cruise and Mr. Toad's Wild Ride. Many of those classics remain today, with a few modernisations, of course. Walt once said, "Disneyland will never be completed. It will continue to grow as long as there is imagination left in the world." Now Disneyland Resort has over 80 attractions, with new lands being added, including Mickey's Toontown in 1993, Disney California Adventure, an accompanying park, which opened in 2001, and Star Wars: Galaxy's Edge in 2019.

But before Disneyland was built, Walt actually had plans to open an amusement park across the street from his studio in Burbank, California. One name he toyed with for this park was none other than "Mickey Mouse Park". Concept drawings for the location, created by Harper Goff, included a few ideas that eventually made it to Disneyland, like a railroad and the presence of water features throughout the park. Now, Walt Disney Animation Studios, a building with Mickey's large sorcerer's hat on top, occupies that land.

Mickey's look at the park has evolved throughout the years. From his earliest park special event appearances, his multifaceted roles have expanded to include performing in parades, shows and celebrations, and appearances at events outside the parks. His wardrobe has expanded, as well – in addition to his favourite tuxedo, Mickey has special show and parade costumes, themed looks for each of the parks, and no trouble finding something to wear for any occasion.

Walt, always looking for the next big idea, set his sights on the next Disneyland, an even larger park with enormous expansion possibilities on the East Coast. On 15 November, 1965, Walt and Roy held a press conference to officially announce the Disney World project.[34] It would open to the public as the Walt Disney World Resort on 1 October, 1971, near Orlando, Florida. Eventually, Disney theme parks would expand internationally, with the opening of Tokyo Disneyland in 1983, Disneyland Paris in 1992, Hong Kong Disneyland in 2005 and Shanghai Disneyland in 2016.

KEY TO PLATE

1: Disneyland Park Fun Map
1958
Mickey Mouse has served as an essential design element at Disneyland since the beginning. "Floral Mickey" which is the first thing visitors see when they enter the park, can be seen towards the bottom centre of the map. Mickey's prominent placement at the top centre of the map suggests his important relationship to the Disneyland experience.

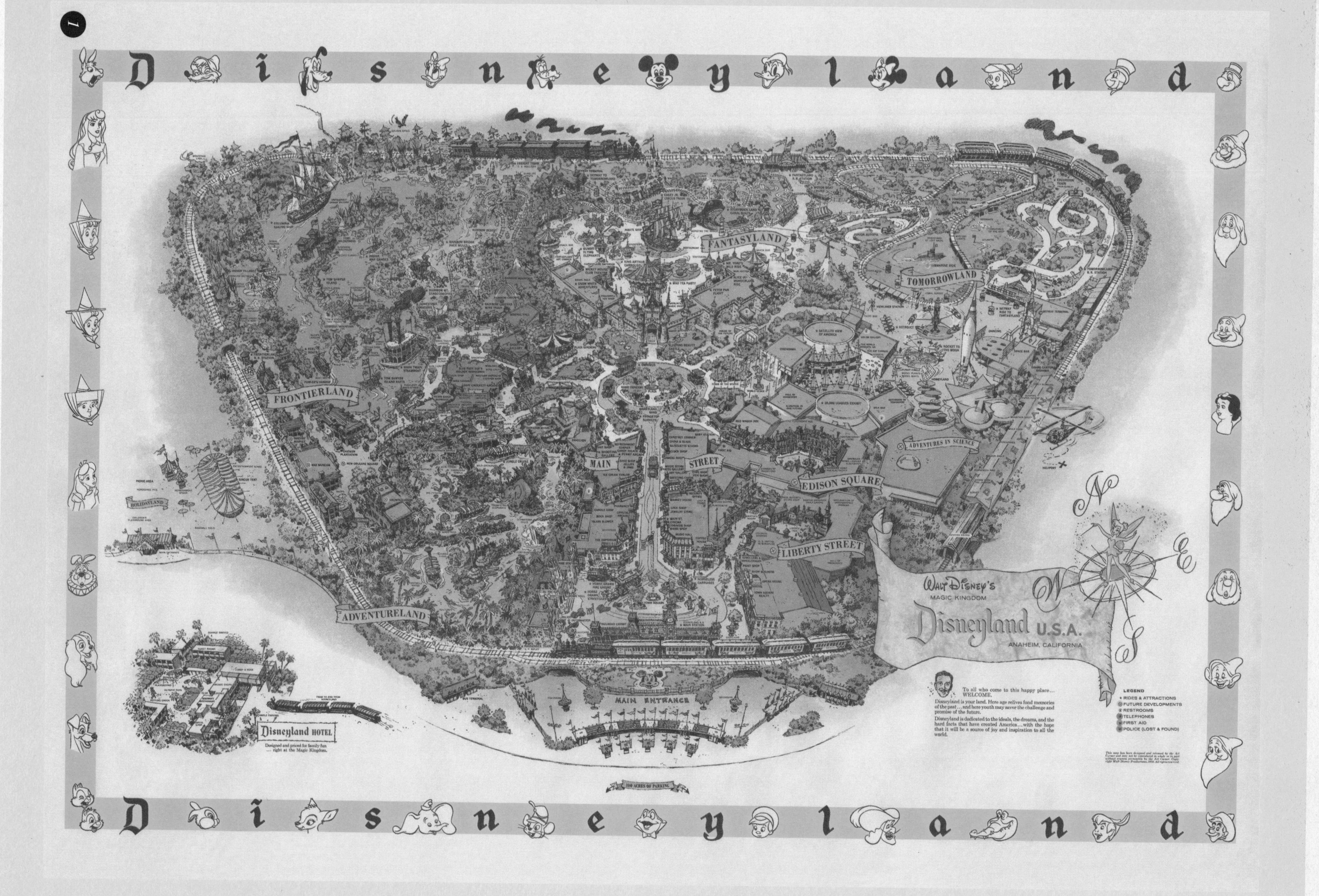
Disneyland
Disneyland
FANTASYLAND
TOMORROWLAND
FRONTIERLAND
MAIN
STREET
EDISON SQUARE
ADVENTURES IN SCIENCE
LIBERTY STREET
ADVENTURELAND
HOLIDAYLAND
MAIN ENTRANCE
100 ACRES OF PARKING
N
E
S
W
WALT DISNEY'S
MAGIC KINGDOM
Disneyland U.S.A.
ANAHEIM, CALIFORNIA
To all who come to this happy place... WELCOME.
Disneyland is your land. Here age relives fond memories of the past... and here youth may savor the challenge and promise of the future.
Disneyland is dedicated to the ideals, the dreams, and the hard facts that have created America... with the hope that it will be a source of joy and inspiration to all the world.
LEGEND
★ RIDES & ATTRACTIONS
FUTURE DEVELOPMENTS
RESTROOMS
TELEPHONES
FIRST AID
POLICE (LOST & FOUND)
This map has been designed and released by the Art Corner and may not be reproduced in whole or in part without express permission by the Art Corner. Copyright Walt Disney Productions, 1958. All rights reserved.
TRAM TO AND FROM DISNEYLAND
AMPLE PARKING
Disneyland HOTEL
Designed and priced for family fun ... right at the Magic Kingdom.

HOLLYWOOD LEGEND

Mickey has always been intertwined with celebrities over the years. Charlie Chaplin, Douglas Fairbanks and Buster Keaton provided the initial inspiration for his storylines and personality in the late 1920s. By the 1930s, actors were being compared to him. In Graham Greene's article in *The Spectator* about Fred Astaire's performance in *Top Hat* he said "Mr Astaire is the nearest approach we are ever likely to have to a human Mickey Mouse."[35] Mickey met future US President John F. Kennedy when he was a child and has even received a kiss on the nose from Oprah.[36] He has met a variety of celebrities including Gigi Hadid, Hugh Jackman, Jessica Lange, Ariana Grande, Chance the Rapper and Channing Tatum, to name a few.

On Mickey's 50th birthday, he was recognised by his peers with a star on the Hollywood Walk of Fame. Mickey was the first cartoon character ever to receive this honour. Minnie was by his side during the ceremony. Her star is across the street from Mickey's in front of the historic El Capitan Theater.

At the 1978 Academy Awards®, the 50th anniversary of the ceremony, Mickey Mouse wore a tuxedo and walked onstage to the "Mickey Mouse March" to present the award for Animated Short Subject with Jodie Foster and Paul Williams. In 1988, Mickey appeared onstage in his *Sorcerer's Apprentice* outfit to present the award for the Best Short Film (Animated) category. He presented with Tom Selleck, a superstar in his own right as the star of *Magnum, P.I.* With a bit of magic, Mickey made the envelope with the name of the winner appear onstage.

In 2003, Mickey was back at the Academy Awards® announcing the winner for Best Animated Short Film and Best Live Action Short Film with actress Jennifer Garner. Mickey Mouse has appeared in 10 films which have been nominated for the Best Animated Short Film category at the Academy Awards®. He won once in this category for *Lend a Paw*.

KEY TO PLATE

1: **Mickey and the Seal**
1948
Mickey and the Seal was nominated for an Academy Award® in 1949.

2: **Mickey's Gala Premiere**
1933
Publicity art adapted from a promotional poster for *Mickey's Gala Premiere* released 1 July, 1933, in which Mickey gets the red carpet rolled out for him at a big Hollywood premiere only to find out it was all a dream. Mickey's 7th birthday was celebrated on 28 September, 1935. In this image, several celebrities including Greta Garbo, Oliver Hardy, Charlie Chaplin and Jimmy Durante wish Mickey a happy birthday.

1

Congratulations Mickey on your Seventh Birthday!

INTERNATIONAL STAR

Whether it is something as small as a stamp, or something as monumental as a Disney park or resort, Mickey is a global cultural icon with recognition around the world. He goes by a variety of names, but he always maintains his signature optimism, and remains in the hearts of children and adults around the globe. In Russia he is Mikki Maus, in Japan, Miki Kuchi, and Topolino in Italy. In China he is Mi Lao Shu and in Sweden he goes by Musse Pigg.

Mickey became known internationally very quickly after *Steamboat Willie* premiered. On 31 December, 1932, the first international Disney children's magazine, *Topolino,* launched in Italy.[37] In 1934, Mickey had his very own magazine *Le Journal de Mickey* in France and a series of Mickey stories published in Spain called *Biblioteca de Aventuras Mickey*.[38] By February 1936, children in the UK were able to enjoy the *Mickey Mouse Magazine* weekly.[39]

By his 7th birthday, Mickey was making an impression on global royalty. King George V insisted that a Mickey Mouse cartoon accompany any movie shown to the British royal family. The Emperor of Japan wore a Mickey Mouse watch. Mickey himself has checked off quite a few global destinations on his passport. In his most recent shorts, Mickey Mouse visits Japan, England, Brazil, Mexico and more international destinations. These Mickey Mouse shorts have been translated into over 30 languages.

At Disneyland Paris, Mickey appears in the show "Mickey and the Magician", to the delight of Parisian visitors. In China at Shanghai Disney Resort, Main Street, U.S.A. was reimagined as Mickey Avenue.[40] And at Hong Kong Disneyland, visitors can see Mickey in 3D at Mickey's PhilharMagic attraction. In Japan, Tokyo Disneyland visitors can meet Mickey and Minnie in person.

For Mickey's 90th birthday celebration, the festivities will be worldwide, including events at Walt Disney Parks and Resorts, such as the World's Biggest Mouse Party. Disney On Ice will tour worldwide with celebrations for Mickey as the "True Original" Disney On Ice host.

KEY TO PLATE

1: **Le Journal de Mickey**
Cover of *Le Journal de Mickey* *circa* 1936.

2: **Los Angeles Times**
This image appears in Section 7 of the 50th Anniversary edition of the *Los Angeles Times,* 4 December, 1931. This art is attributed to Floyd Gottfredson. Section 7 was dedicated solely to the film industry.

3: **Nel Regno di Topolino**
Cover of *Nel Regno di Topolino*, an Italian Magazine circa 1935.

1

To The Press *of the* World
MICKEY MOUSE
extends appreciation for
the wondrous words of
praise bestowed on his
humble efforts to add to
the gaiety of nations --

WALT DISNEY

2

3

MICKEY AT WAR

About one year after the premiere of *Fantasia*, the United States formally entered World War II with the attack on Pearl Harbor. This brought production at The Walt Disney Studios to a crawl, as their resources needed to be directed towards the war effort. The impact of the war was felt immediately, as The Walt Disney Studios were suddenly occupied by military personnel.

During this time, only two Mickey Mouse cartoons were released, *Mickey's Birthday Party* and *Symphony Hour*, both in 1942. But Mickey and his friends did not disappear, they were used on Civil Defense posters, which encouraged Americans to aid in the war effort whether they were conserving gas, keeping patriotic information within the American borders or purchasing war bonds to help support war-effort funds. Throughout the war, more than 90 percent of production at Disney Studios was related to World War II.[41]

Mickey and his friends also appeared on over 1,200 designs for military insignia produced by the studio. Military units could write to the Disney studio to have insignias created for them. Nearly every request that was received was attended to. Without television, information was disseminated to the public through newspapers, the radio or in movie theatres. During this time, Donald, Pluto and Goofy appeared in shorts created to educate the American public on the current situation while comforting them with familiar faces. Americans were fearful of another attack on US soil, so seeing a beloved cartoon character would have been a moment of reprieve.

KEY TO PLATE

1: Wartime poster
1942
Volunteers with the Aircraft Warning Service searched for planes flying into America starting in May 1941. Civilians were also encouraged to take part in the effort thanks to Mickey.

2: Miltary insignia
1942
An image like this may have appeared on an aircraft worker's jacket or pinback button. The items Mickey is holding form a "V" for "Victory".

3: Civil Defense poster
1943
During World War II, fuel was rationed in the United States. Posters like this one featuring Mickey, Donald and Goofy reminded civilians to share cars whenever possible.

4: Civil Defense poster
circa 1942-1945
This poster encourages soldiers to keep knowledge within their units.

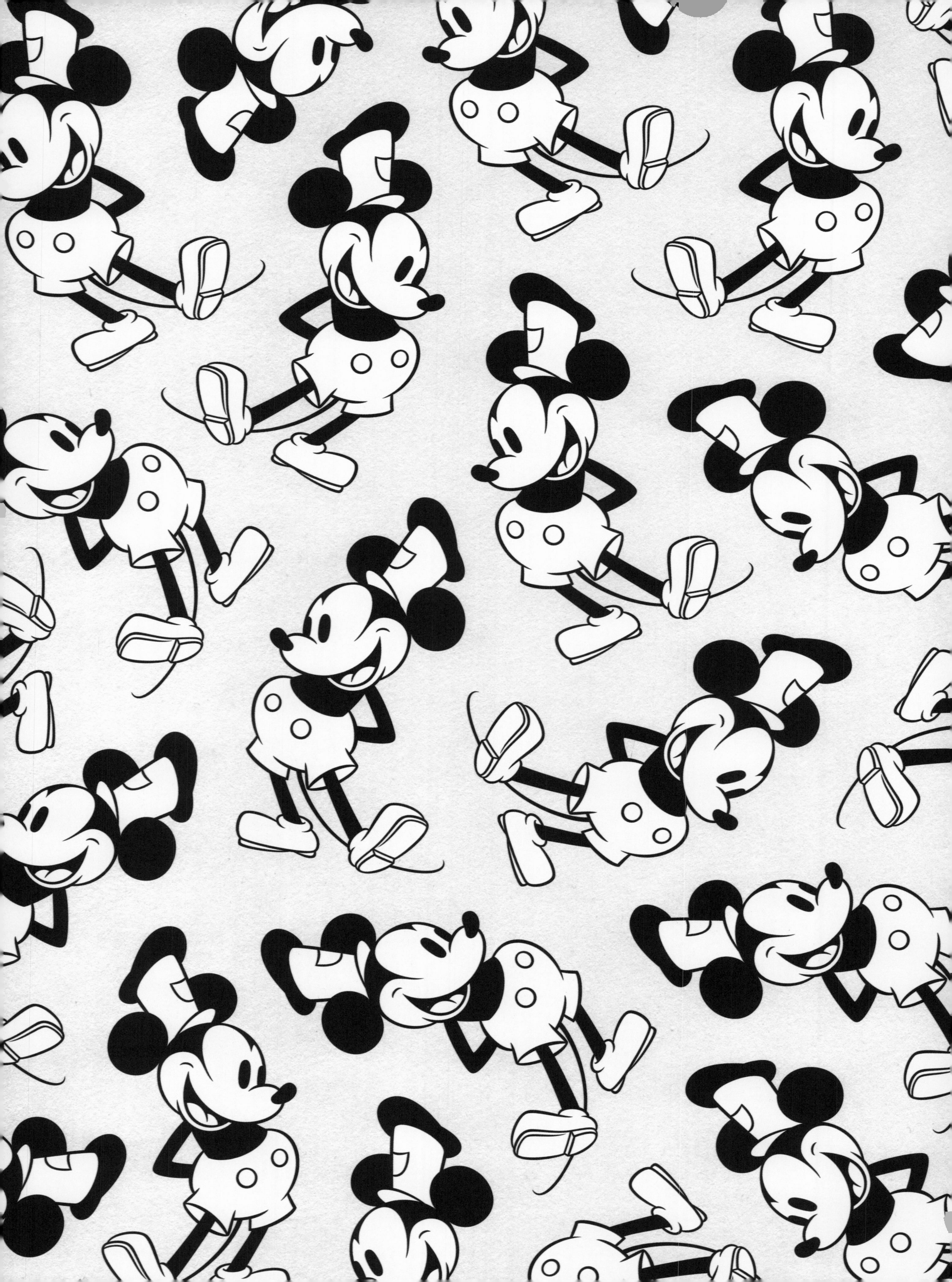

SECTION 7

A PLACE IN OUR HEARTS

Death of Walt Disney
Public Reactions to Mickey
The Ultimate Pop Culture Icon

DEATH OF WALT DISNEY

On 15 December, 1966, Walter Elias Disney passed away at 65 years of age. He left behind a legacy of over 600 films, countless characters and more than 30 Academy Awards®. At Disneyland, the flag was lowered. According to the *Los Angeles Times*, his family requested that any donations be made to the California Institute of the Arts, a college Roy and Walt helped to form in 1961, which has since boasted graduates including Tim Burton, Brad Bird and Sofia Coppola.[42]

In an interview with *McCall's* titled "I Live with a Genius", three years before his passing, Lillian Disney said of Walt, "He has been compared to Leonardo da Vinci as an artist and to La Fontaine, the great writer of fables. One of the originals from *Snow White* hangs in the Metropolitan Museum in New York. The *Encyclopedia Britannica* devotes a chapter to Mickey Mouse. These things aren't accidents, any more than Walt Disney's success is accidental. He works hard, he has high standards of taste, and he will never compromise. But applause goes in one ear and out the other. Past triumphs bore him; he is always too busy with future schemes."

After his death, several of Walt's "future schemes" would live on to become reality, some sooner than others. In his *New York Times* obituary, his brother Roy is quoted as saying, "We will continue to operate Walt's company in the way that he had established and guided it. All of the plans for the future that Walt had begun will continue to move ahead." Walt's dreams, including what would become of the Walt Disney World Resort, and a theme park drawing heavy inspiration from his EPCOT (Experimental Prototype Community of Tomorrow) concept, would ultimately see the light of day in 1971 and 1982 respectively, helping to forever change the themed entertainment industry.

Walt's obituary in the *Los Angeles Times* ends with a quote from him that reads, "That's the principal thing that I hope to leave when I move on to greener pastures," he said. "If I can provide a place to develop talent of the future, I think I will have accomplished something."[43]

KEY TO PLATE

1: LA Herald Examiner
Karl Hubenthal for the *LA. Herald Examiner*, December 1966.

PUBLIC REACTIONS TO MICKEY

From the beginning, children had a place in their hearts for Mickey. In the *New York Times* on 25 September, 1938, it was reported on Mickey's 10th birthday that "thousands of telegrams will be sent to Mickey to the Hollywood studio from all over the world, as they have in the past [...] 'including one from President Roosevelt.'"

Walt's legacy is continually recognised with posthumous awards and in 2009, Diane Disney Miller founded The Walt Disney Family Museum, which continues to honour Walt's legacy. Through Lillian Disney's efforts, The Walt Disney Concert Hall, designed by renowned architect Frank Gehry, opened in 2003 as a symbol of Walt's devotion to the arts and Los Angeles. In 1993, Blaine Gibson designed the bronze Partners Statue, in which Walt holds Mickey's hand. This statue welcomes guests at Disneyland, Magic Kingdom Park at Walt Disney World, Tokyo Disneyland, Walt Disney Studios Paris and The Walt Disney Studios lot in California.

Mickey has won a lasting place in the hearts of the public and is remembered across generations. In the public eye, he stands for childhood comfort, optimism, and heart. Although his design has changed throughout the years, he has remained instantly recognisable.

KEY TO PLATE

1: ***Charlotte Clark Mickey Mouse doll***
Walt Disney standing next to a Charlotte Clark Mickey Mouse doll posing on top of a pile of fan mail. Reportedly, Mickey would receive up to 800,000 letters a year.[44]

THE ULTIMATE POP CULTURE ICON

Aside from being the symbol of one of the largest media and entertainment companies in the world, Mickey Mouse is an icon that has remained culturally relevant. The classic Mickey Mouse ear hats have graced the heads of celebrities such as Tina Fey, Lady Gaga, SJP, Beyoncé, Emma Watson, Twiggy, Madonna, Rihanna and Katie Perry. The headwear even makes an appearance in the iconic original *Rocky Horror Picture Show* film, as worn by the character Columbia. Sheldon from *The Big Bang Theory* has a pair of ears and Showtime's Dexter also has sported the look.

In popular movies, Mickey Mouse references are abundant, with noticeable moments being mentioned in *James Bond: Spectre* and *Indiana Jones: The Last Crusade*. He even appears on Robert Langdon's watch in the *Da Vinci Code* series.

Mentions of Mickey in music lyrics include David Bowie's "Life on Mars" and Prince's "Dance On". His presence in lyrics remains relevant, with appearances in the lyrics for Alabama Shakes' "Miss You" from 2015. Originally recorded by Cole Porter in 1934, "You're the Top" features Mickey and has been covered by legends such as Louis Armstrong, Barbara Streisand, Ella Fitzgerald and Frank Sinatra, to name but a few.

An inspiration to international fashion designers, including Marc Jacobs, Fred Segal and Jeremy Scott, Mickey fashion continues to evolve. Mickey even graced a shirt in one of John Lennon's iconic photographs.

In the art scene, Mickey has held his ground since his gallery debut in New York at the Kennedy Galleries in 1933.[45] He has inspired pieces by artists such as Andy Warhol, Roy Lichtenstein, Thomas Hart Benton and many others. For his 50th birthday, Mickey short films were screened at The Museum of Modern Art for several weeks. In an article for *The New York Times*, Richard Oldenburg, the director of the museum, said: "Mickey Mouse represented a kind of simple classic design that has an effect on many of the visual arts."[46]

KEY TO PLATE

1: Mickey Mouse artwork by Andy Warhol

This image is one of 10 screen prints done for the "Myths Portfolio" series Warhol created in 1981. Measuring a square 96.5 centimetres, each screen printing is sprinkled with diamond dust, giving it a sparkling hue. Other icons who appear in this series include Santa Claus, Superman, Greta Garbo and Uncle Sam. Developed towards the end of Warhol's career, this piece cemented Mickey in the pop art world.

GALERIE KAMMER

Februar - März 1982 · Böhmersweg 9 · Hamburg 13 · Telefon 45 94 27

SECTION 8

90 YEARS ON

Mickey Reimagined
A Glimpse into the Future

MICKEY REIMAGINED

On 5 May, 2006, Mickey entered into the world of regularly scheduled computer-generated television animation with his appearance in *Mickey Mouse Clubhouse* on the Disney Channel. He starred alongside Minnie, Goofy, Donald, Daisy and Pluto in this preschool television show. Minnie Mouse also got the computer-generated animation treatment with her own show called *Minnie's Bow-Toons* which premiered 14 November, 2011. The show, inspired by an episode of *Mickey Mouse Clubhouse*, is about a bow and bow-tie shop run by Daisy and Minnie.

In 2003, the year of Mickey's 75th birthday, Mickey appeared for one of the first times in 3D in Mickey's PhilharMagic, an attraction in Magic Kingdom Park at Walt Disney World Resort. *Mickey's Twice Upon a Christmas*, released on video on 9 November, 2004 was the first entirely computer-generated Mickey animation released on video.

On 27 November, 2013, a Mickey short called *Get a Horse!* appeared before the theatrical release of *Frozen*. The short made history as the first solo directing credit for a woman on a feature-length cartoon. To achieve a vintage feel, archival recordings of Walt's voice were used for Mickey Mouse. The short is mostly animated in 2D black-and-white until characters break through the screen, tumbling into a colourful 3D world.

New, original Mickey Mouse shorts have been airing on the Disney Channel since the summer of 2013, taking Mickey and his gang on a variety of adventures around the world. The creator of the show, Paul Ruddish, said, "It was really just thinking about my favourite Mickey Mouse cartoons and where Mickey had been in all of his evolutions along the way. I always gravitated back to the rubber hose stuff from the late '20s, early '30s and would always stop at the Main Street [Cinema] at Disneyland and watch *Plane Crazy*. I loved how zany and surreal those old cartoons were and how mischievous Mickey was, while still being naïve and good-spirited." Over 90 shorts in this series have been created to date.

KEY TO PLATE

1: Scene from Get a Horse!
27 November, 2013
Mickey uses his leg as a staircase for Minnie. This animation was hand-drawn in the rubber hose style of the 1928 classic Mickey cartoons.

2: Peg Leg Pete crashes into Mickey and Horace Horsecollar, almost causing them to push through the screen
Get a Horse! was nominated for an Academy Award® in the Best Animated Short Film category.

3: Peg Leg Pete pushes Mickey through the screen into the 3D world of colour
The hole Mickey is pushed out from can be seen on Peg Leg Pete's left cheek. From this point on, the animation is simultaneous 2D and 3D.

4: Mickey transforms Horace Horsecollar into an aeroplane, reminiscent of Plane Crazy
Mickey and Horace fly into the audience until they bounce off the screen.

5: Peg Leg Pete and Minnie Mouse get submerged in water
Mickey uses his tail as a pin to poke a hole in the screen, allowing the water to escape into the 3D world.

1

2

3
4
5

A GLIMPSE INTO THE FUTURE

Mickey has always embraced the newest technologies, whether it was synchronised sound in the late 1920s, colour animation in the mid-1930s, stereophonic sound in the 1940s or television in the 1950s. As technology advances, so too will Mickey, while also staying true to his character, of course.

At Disney Parks, the World's Biggest Mouse Party celebrates Mickey and Minnie's 90 years across Disney Parks around the world. Opening Ceremony hosted a runway show at Disneyland in spring 2018 featuring couture Mickey-inspired designs for Mickey's 90th birthday. And Mickey & Minnie's Runaway Railway, the first Mickey-themed ride-through attraction, is coming to Disney's Hollywood Studios near Orlando. The attraction that ties into the contemporary Mickey Mouse shorts has a new theme song and allows riders to enter a Mickey Mouse cartoon short and see where the adventure takes them.

Mickey's lengthy career will always inform new ideas, whether it's tapping into the pie-eye design of the 1930s in his current shorts or his enduring love for Minnie. In an article titled "What Mickey Means to Me", Walt wrote: "But all we ever intended for him was that he should make people everywhere chuckle with him and at him." Whether Mickey enters the world of virtual reality or robotics, that sentiment will be revisited by the new animators and artists who continue to expand Mickey's universe. No matter what the future holds, Mickey will continue to inspire people of all ages around the world.

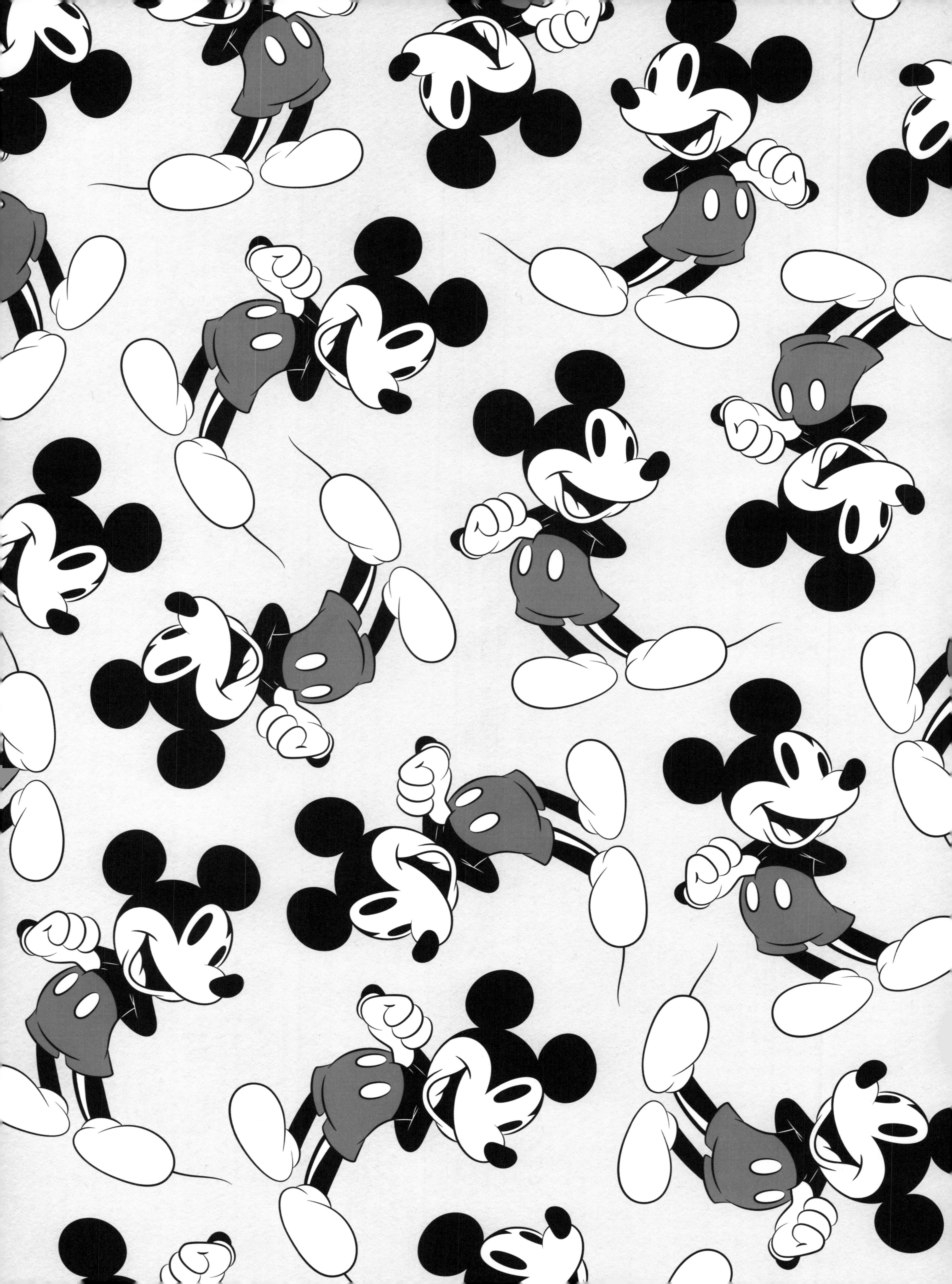

SECTION 9

LIBRARY

INDEX

ART CREDITS

Pages 48-49:
"Mickey Mouse Meets Konrad Lorenz". 1979. From Natural History, May 1979. Image © Walt Disney Productions.

Page 71:
Hubenthal, Karl. "Walt Disney Orbit". 1966. Reproduced with permission from the Estate of Karl Hubenthal.

Page 74:
Warhol, Andy. 1982. 'Mickey Mouse'. © 2018 The Andy Warhol Foundation for the Visual Arts, Inc. / Licensed by DACS, London.

REFERENCES

1 Apgar, G. 2015. *Mickey Mouse: Emblem of the American Spirit.* San Francisco: The Walt Disney Family Foundation Press, pp. 28.

2 Apgar, G. 2014. *A Mickey Mouse Reader.* Jackson: University Press of Mississippi, pp. 234.

3 Gabler, N. 2006. *Walt Disney: The Triumph of the American Imagination.* New York: Knopf, pp. 102.

4 Walt Disney Family Museum, 2012. "The Birth of a Mouse." Available at: https://www.waltdisney.org/blog/birth-mouse

5 Apgar, G. 2015, pp. 114.

6 Apgar, G. 2014, pp. 38-39.

7 Ibid. pp. 179.

8 Gabler, N. 2006, pp. 117.

9 Apgar, G. 2014, pp. 28.

10 Gabler, N. 2006, pp. 105.

11 Walt Disney Family Museum, 2013. "Mickey's First Love: Minnie." Available at: https://www.waltdisney.org/blog/mickeys-first-love-minnie

12 Apgar, G. 2015, pp. 72.

13 *Motion Picture Herald*, 1932. "Mickey Mouse's Fourth Birthday." 1 October. Available at: https://www.dix-project.net/item/2084/motion-picture-herald-issue-109-1-mickey-mouse-s-fourth-birthday

14 Gabler, N. 2006, pp. 141.

15 Apgar, G. 2015, pp. 116.

16 Gabler, N. 2006, pp. 198.

17 Apgar, G. 2014, pp. 120.

18 Gabler, N. 2006, pp. 141.

19 Apgar, G. 2014, pp. 120.

20 Gottfredson, F. 2011. *Walt Disney's Mickey Mouse Vol. 2: Trapped on Treasure Island.* Seattle, WA: Fantagraphics Books, pp. 281.

21 Russell, H. 1937. "L'Affaire Mickey Mouse." *New York Times Magazine*, 26 December.

22 United States Postal Service, 2008. "Limited Edition 'Art of Disney Stamp' Book Reveals Back Story of Most Popular Stamp Series of All-Time." Available at: http://about.usps.com/news/national-releases/2008pr08_127.htm

23 Finch, C. 2004. *The Art of Walt Disney: From Mickey Mouse to the Magic Kingdoms.* New York: Harry N. Abrams. pp. 82.

24 Apgar, G. 2014, pp. 168.

25 Heide, R., Gilman, J., Peterson, M. and White, P. 2001. *Mickey Mouse: The Evolution, the Legend, the Phenomenon!* New York: Disney Editions, pp. 65.

26 Apgar, G. 2015, pp. 129.

27 Gabler, N. 2006, pp. 316.

28 Gabler, N. 2006, pp. 522.

29 Burr, L., 1990. "My TV Dinner With Mickey: Television: 'The Mickey Mouse Club' debuted 35 years ago today. The author, a Mouseketeer, talks about its impact." *LA Times*, 3 October. Available at: http://articles.latimes.com/1990-10-03/entertainment/ca-1525_1_mickey-mouse-club

30 Gabler, N. 2006, pp. 522.

31 Ibid, pp. 522.

32 Maslin, J. 1990. "Mickey Plays the Palace, and Rescuers Go Walkabout." *The New York Times*, 16 Nov. Available at: https://www.nytimes.com/1990/11/16/movies/review-film-mickey-plays-the-palace-and-rescuers-go-walkabout.html

33 Apgar, G. 2014, pp. 301.

34 Finch, C. 2004, pp. 445.

35 Apgar, G. 2014, pp. 80.

36 Apgar, G. 2015, pp. 12.

37 Ibid, pp. 152.

38 Ibid, pp. 142.

39 Ibid, pp. 152.

40 Lasky, J. 2017. "At Shanghai Disney Resort, Mulan, Mickey and Dumplings." *New York Times*, 4 July. Available at: https://www.nytimes.com/2017/07/04/travel/disneyland-shanghai-theme-parks.html

41 Walt Disney Family Museum, 2011. "Walt Disney Joins the War Effort." Available at: https://www.waltdisney.org/blog/walt-disney-joins-war-effort-celebrate-us-111111

42 Trimborn, H. 1966. "Wizard of Fantasy Walt Disney Dies." *LA Times*, 16 December. Available at: http://www.latimes.com/local/obituaries/archives/la-me-walt-disney-19661216-story.html

43 Ibid.

44 Apgar, G. 2014, pp. 87.

45 Ibid, pp.72.

46 Quindlen, A. 1978. "Mouse Museum Celebrate Mickey." *New York Times*, 17 November. Available at: https://www.nytimes.com/1978/11/17/archives/modern-museum-celebrates-mickey-a-career-of-five-decades.html